ETHIOPIA UNBOUND:
STUDIES IN RACE EMANCIPATION

ETHIOPIA UNBOUND:
STUDIES IN RACE EMANCIPATION

J. CASELY HAYFORD

FIRST PUBLISHED 1911.
THIS CENTENNIAL EDITION IS
PUBLISHED ON THE OCCASION OF
ITS 100TH ANNIVERSARY

Black Classic Press
Baltimore

ETHIOPIA UNBOUND:
STUDIES IN RACE EMANCIPATION

Library of Congress Control Number: 2004116442
ISBN: 978-1-58073-010-5
Cover image: Ethiopia Awakening sculpture
by Meta Vaux Warrick Fuller

Printed by BCP Digital Printing,
an affiliate company of Black Classic Press, Inc.

To review or purchase Black Classic Press books, visit:
www.blackclassicbooks.com

You may also obtain a list of titles by writing to:
Black Classic Press
c/o List
P.O. Box 13414
Baltimore, MD 21203

Ethiopia Unbound:
Studies in Race Emancipation

Introduction

Molefi Kete Asante

One hundred years ago, Ekra-Agiman, writing under the name of Joseph Ephraim Casely Hayford, published the powerful book *Ethiopia Unbound: Studies in Race Emancipation* in 1911. Publication of this work immediately established Casely Hayford as one of the leading African thinkers of his generation. Born in the part of Africa that the British called the Gold Coast, today's Ghana, Casely Hayford was Fante by birth and African by nature. Of course, because of his training in the best traditions of the European world, he ventured to see himself as a universal intellectual by sentiment. He had been born on September 29, 1866, into one of the prominent Fante families of the Gold Coast.

Casely Hayford was the fourth son of Reverend and Mrs. Joseph de Graft Hayford. The Hayford family was one of the leading Fante families on the Atlantic Coast, having made its money from trading with the Europeans. After attending the Wesleyan Boy's High School at Cape Coast, Casely Hayford was sent to college at Fourah Bay in Sierra Leone. It was the leading institution of higher learning in

West Africa. At 23 years of age he returned to the Gold Coast and became the principal of Accra Wesleyan High School. He subsequently worked for James Hutton Brew, his uncle, on the newspaper *Gold Coast Echo*. He soon traveled to England and managed to obtain his law degree from Cambridge. He was called to the bar in 1896 and then returned to the Gold Coast as an attorney. Casely Hayford proved that he had a brilliant legal mind, capable of having mastered all of the legal theory of the British as well as being grounded in his own Fante law. Indeed, prior to writing *Ethiopia Unbound* he had written the definitive work on the customs of his region under the title *Gold Coast Native Institutions*.

Sometimes a book enters a political and social context as if it were a child that had been called into being to answer some particular situation either immediately or at some future date. *Ethiopia Unbound* is a veritable tour de force of African intellectual sensibilities. Although not as widely read as W. E. B. DuBois' *The Soul of Black Folk*, *Ethiopia Unbound* proved its own mettle as a paramount achievement of the Black intelligentsia. Casely Hayford was every bit the genius that DuBois was when it came to the question of defending the race against the worst forms of Eurocentric irrationality.

Ethiopia Unbound has its own aura of greatness, and while it has not been read as often as it should have been by African Americans I hope that the re-publication of the work brings it the deserved review and analysis that it should have among the progressive minds of Africa's children and others who struggle for human liberation. The book is an exercise in support of African culture in the face of a dominating Western ethos. Casely Hayford is able to praise the Japanese example that he sees as one the African people should take. Japan appeared to maintain its own traditional culture while modernizing itself; Casely

Hayford argues that Africa could follow that example. There is some bending, however, in Casely Hayford's argument because he manages to assert African culture while remaining deeply entrenched in the Methodist Christian ideology of his colonial training.

Ethiopia Unbound is subtitled *Studies in Race Emancipation* during a time that the European colonial powers sought to bring into being their permanent occupation of the African continent. The Berlin Conference had been held under the watchful eye of Von Bismarck of Germany and Leopold of Belgium in 1884–1885 with 13 white nations assembled for the dismemberment of the mother continent. No African leader or representative sat at the Berlin meeting; such was the arrogance of power. Within 30 years, Nehanda and Kaguvi would stand up to the British in Zimbabwe; the Asante nation would challenge the British on several fronts; the Ethiopians, under the leadership of Menelik II, would defeat the Italians at Adwa; Africans would rise up in numerous violent protests and struggles against all occupiers; DuBois would publish *The Souls of Black Folk*; and Casely Hayford would write *Ethiopia Unbound,* literally taking his title and subtitle from the intense moral, physical, and social ferment of the time. No one ever wrote a more moving account of the African reaction to racism, oppression, and abuse. In his book, Casely Hayford asserted African humanity and intelligence in the face of the most abject morality and stubborn ignorance of Europeans. His aim was to object to the cornering of Africans in the category of primitive, and in his objection Casely Hayford took every opportunity to reject European superiority claims.

There was something pre-Afrocentric about *Ethiopia Unbound*. While the book has its moments when the author is seeking to show that Africans are comparable to Europeans, something that was unnecessary to demonstrate, it also has examples where the writer asserts African culture without regard to Europe. These are the best instances of African agency. In fact, the idea is really that Europe does not have to authenticate Africa, and all of his life Casely Hayford worked to demonstrate this fact. His books grew out of the same philosophical soil as his politics; he was pro-African, indeed, pro-Fante.

One can clearly see, however, that his acceptance of his own culture did not hinder him in his Pan-African aspirations. In this regard, he was a disciple of Edward Wilmot Blyden and a practitioner of African cultural universalism.

Several aspects of Casely Hayford's work strike the interested reader. His breadth of historical and philosophical knowledge of the European and African worlds is extraordinary for his time. He is clearly in the top class of thinkers about matters of morality and humanity in his age. More than many others, especially more than the European thinkers, he brings to the table African and European ideas and is able to move between them with an ease that shows him to be a man of vast learning. What is more is that it is not just his intelligence and awareness of philosophies, traditions, and histories of the world that attracts the reader but his sincere and passionate desire to see a more morally correct world.

In some ways Casely Hayford is trying to balance his traditional Akan and Fante history and philosophy with his acquired Christian sentiments. He is more successful than most, but no African could ever reconcile the traditions to Christianity successfully. They are two separate ways of looking at the world. Whatever he tries to do with the Fante God, Nyiakrapon, he cannot make this deity the same as the Christian deity. However, Casely Hayford establishes himself clearly in the same realm of knowledge as the Europeans by introducing us early in the book to a character he calls Silas Whitely, obviously a white man from London. Whitely is interested in some of the intellectual ideas that challenge Casely Hayford's alter ego who is called Kwamankra, clearly an Akan name. Of course, Kwamankra is perhaps better educated than Silas Whitely in the ways of Whitely's people and, consequently, is always his better when it comes to rational arguments or arguments from the European classics.

Hayford moves Kwamankra through his university days in England to marriage to Mansa, who dies in childbirth. He is left a single man to bring up his remaining child. He is seen living the life of a barrister in the old colonial Gold Coast, assisting any of his brothers and sisters that he can to live creatively in the midst of European dominance and oppression. Of course, such an educated and intelligent Black man would almost immediately run afoul of the local colonial overseers who were no match for Kwamankra, either intellectually or spiritually. Casely Hayford shows the decrepit moral condition of the whites who occupy the Gold Coast, their wanton disregard for the local rulers, their insolence, their arrogance in the face of overwhelming and recognizable facts contrary to their beliefs, and their drunkenness and lascivious behavior. They were not nearly the men that Kwamankra showed himself to be.

Silas Whitely eventually moves to the Gold Coast as the colonial chaplain and is immediately embroiled in a dispute over whether or not a cemetery should be segregated. He chooses the side of the racist whites who want to see the graves segregated. Whitely and Kwamankra appear as strangers whose earlier contact in London is not referred to in any special manner. They had both chosen their sides in the struggle over race and domination. Kwamankra is committed to his African culture. Whitely never appears again in the text.

At the top of the 20th century, Casely Hayford wanted to demonstrate the contradictions in the Christian religion as it pertained to the British administrators of the Gold Coast. In many respects this was a futile exercise that had been used in the African community for nearly 100 years when in 1829 David Walker wrote in his *Appeal to the Colored Citizens of the World* that the white Christian Americans were the worst humans ever put on earth. It is this same argument that attracts Casely Hayford, and he is intent on showing that the white man was not better in morality than the Black man. Indeed, as far as he could see, the Black man was superior to the white in matters of human relations.

Several important members of the African intelligentsia enter Casely Hayford's discourse in various ways. He is drawn to remark on the likes of Edward Wilmot Blyden, W. E. B. DuBois, and Booker T. Washington, the men of ideas of his generation. But it is Blyden that he loves and believes in and follows in many dimensions. Who is Edward Wilmot Blyden?

Blyden was born in the Virgin Islands and found himself to be one of the leading intellectuals of Liberia, with profound ideas about African culture. As an author, he was without a peer in his age, having written immensely popular works defending African culture and projecting an authentic African voice in the midst of religious inroads from Islam and Christianity. He was elevated in the mind of Casely Hayford and seen as perhaps the African race's greatest giant since the days of Frederick Douglass. Blyden had written on many subjects and was an expert in the languages of Europe and Africa. His massive tome, *Christianity and Islam in Africa*, was received as one of the best sociological and anthropological examinations of its time. He exerted influence on many intellectuals, preachers, teachers, and race leaders who wanted to see

Africa free of colonialism. He was a towering figure of exceptional insight in Hayford's opinion.

On the other hand Hayford did not share the same opinion of the young DuBois who had burst upon the scene of African scholarship and commentary with several books by the time of *Ethiopia Unbound*. Of course, Du Bois would live for another 70 years or so, and had Casely Hayford lived as long he might have had more favorable comments about DuBois' work. His criticism of DuBois in *The Souls of Black Folk* is the same criticism that has been lodged against his double consciousness theory.

When I gave my first written criticism of double consciousness in the book *The Lure and Loathing* I had not read Casely Hayford, yet he reached the same conclusion I would reach 80 years later. There could never be double consciousness; it is a false concept.

As DuBois repelled Casely Hayford for his confusion, Hampton College attracted him for its possibilities. He saw in Hampton the dream of Kwamankra: to have a Pan African university where students would truly learn African philosophy and culture, and laugh with joy because of the promise of the future. In this respect, Casely Hayford is an optimist, always hoping for an African university that he could return to with all of his Western education and demonstrates how Africans could achieve at the highest levels while maintaining the values of the Fante people.

This book is extraordinary in its optimism. One could approach the book as a novel, a philosophical treatise, a dialogue of rationalism, an Edwardian romance, or as a meditation on love of self, family, and community. It is all of these and more because it is filled with African as well as Greek myths as reference points and is a sound political tract on the contemporary strivings of the Turks and the

Russians as well as African life under British colonia rule. Yet Casely Hayford is certain in the end that there would be victory over the colonial oppression in the Gold Coast and that his people, the Fante, would enjoy their own freedoms and independence as citizens equal to any in the world. For him, this is not just the objective of the Fante, it is the aim for the entire Ethiopian world, by which he means all of Africa. "Rise, you mighty giant! Rise! Ethiopia will soon be unbound!" And so it was.

M.K. Asante

TO THE SONS OF ETHIOPIA

THE WORLD WIDE OVER.

CONTENTS.

A GLOSSARY.

—.... ....—

Omanhin . . . . Head of a state or king, plural *Amanhin*.

Kruba . . . . . A vessel for carrying light articles; in this case for collecting money.

Nanamu . . . . The gods of the Fantis.

Nanamu-Krome . The abodes of the gods.

Sanko Songs . . Sea songs.

Wonkora wonkor . Without whom not, an idiom signifying Leader of Leaders.

Effua Kobi . . . The Mother of Calcali, King of Ashanti, before the war of 1873.

_____

"DO NOT BELIEVE THAT YOU KNOW A
PEOPLE IF YOU HAVE NOT ASCENDED TO
THEIR GODS."—M. Edgar Quinet.

_____

ETHIOPIA UNBOUND.

CHAPTER I.

An Ethiopian Conservative.

At the dawn of the twentieth century, men of
light and leading both in Europe and in America
had not yet made up their minds as to what place
to assign to the spiritual aspirations of the black
man; and the Nations were casting about for an
answer to the wail which went up from the heart
of the oppressed race for opportunity. And
yet it was at best but an impotent cry. For there
has never lived a people worth writing about who
have not shaped out a destiny for themselves, or
carved out their own opportunity.

Before this time, however, it had been dis-
covered that the black man was not necessarily
the missing link between man and ape. It had
even been granted that for intellectual endowments he had nothing to be ashamed of in an
open competition with the Aryan or any other

type. Here was a being anatomically perfect, adaptive and adaptable to any and every sphere of the struggle for life. Sociologically, he had succeeded in recording upon the pages of contemporary history a conception of family life unknown to Western ideas. Moreover, he was the scion of a spiritual sphere peculiar unto himself; for when Western Nations would have exhausted their energy in the vain struggle for the things which satisfy not, it was felt that it would be to these people to whom the world would turn for inspiration, seeing that in them only would be found those elements which make for pure altruism, the leaven of all human experience.

Again, the art of the caricaturist had by now been played out. It was no longer possible, as far as this race was concerned, to depict the Sultan of Zanzibar, for example, other than as an Ethiopian gentleman, "clothed and in his right mind."

And there were sons of God among them, men whom the Gods visited as of yore; for even now three continents were ringing with the names of men like Du Bois, Booker T. Washington, Blyden, Dunbar, Coleridge Taylor, and others—men who had distinguished themselves in the fields of activity and intellectuality—and it was by no means an uncommon thing to meet in the

universities of Europe and America the sons of
Ethiopia in quest of the golden tree of knowledge.
Here, in London, about the time of which we
write, were to be seen two young men, walking
arm in arm up Tottenham Court Road, and, ever
and anon, stopping to examine old dirty books in
some second-class bookstall, or some quaint relics
in a curiosity shop.

Presently, the twain stopped at a particularly
ancient looking bookshop off a by-street leading
to Upper Bedford Place. The darker man of the
two picked up from the stall outside, a well-
thumbed copy of Marcus Aurelius, and began
carelessly to turn over the leaves. Suddenly he
stopped, and his face grew pensive. Turning to
his friend, he said, " Isn't it funny, Whitely, the
remarkable similarity of thought and almost of
expression there is between all the great teachers
of the past? Listen to what, for instance,
Marcus Aurelius says here," reading aloud a
paragraph from the *Meditations*, which ran thus:
" ' Pray not to save thy child, but that thou
mayest not fear to lose him.' Now, you, a
Divinity student, what do you make of that? "
And without waiting for an answer, he added,
" Does it not read very much like the teaching of
the holy Nazarene—' He that findeth his life shall
lose it,' or words to that effect? Now, what I

wish to know is what had Jesus Christ in common with Marcus Aurelius? "

" Candidly, Kwamankra," said Whitely, " I have never given the matter a thought; but since you put the question, and viewing it from a merely debatable standpoint, I am inclined to say that the first question to consider is whether Jesus Christ was man or God."

Kwamankra raised his eyes in astonishment. " You do surprise me, Whitely; how can you, of all others, have any doubt upon the matter? I thought you were going up for Orders."

Whitely appeared confused, but soon regaining composure, he said to his companion, " Let us move on."

As they sauntered along, Whitely began : " You know, Kwamankra, I can talk better walking, and I will now answer the question you put to me a while ago. At one time I thought of taking Orders, and even now I may do so. But a little evil thing in the shape of an unanswerable doubt haunts me by day and night, and it is even the self-same question I put to you at the book shop."

" Well, I hardly know what to say, Whitely. In these matters I, of course, regard myself as an outsider. You see we pagans come all the way here to sit at the feet of Gamaliel," he said with a little mischievous laugh, " and it is uncommonly hard upon us for you to entertain doubts upon the broad questions upon which we seek comparison and light. But I can conceive of no such difficulty as you experience in our system. Jesus Christ man or God?" he repeated slowly and musingly unto himself—then turning somewhat suddenly to his friend, he said, "You know, Whitely, since I learnt your language, not as a vehicle of thought, but as a means of more intimately studying your philosophy, I have been trying to get at the root idea of the word 'God'; and so far as my researches have gone, it is an Anglo-Saxon word, the Teutonic form being *Gutha*, which is said to be quite distinct from 'good.' Whence then, one may ask, come your ideas, as associated with the fountain of all good, of omnipresence, omniscience, omnipotence? Of course they are borrowed from the Romans, who were pagans like ourselves, and who, indeed, had much to learn from the Ethiopians through the Greeks."

A turn or two took the young men to Russell Square, and soon they found themselves at Bedford Place. The darker man of the two produced a latch-key, and invited his companion to come in. There was nothing remarkable about the rooms except that they were furnished in the Oriental style. Here and there, at convenient corners, were divans with rich cushions, embroidered in silk, and carpets of leopard skins into which the feet sank as one walked. On the walls were trophies, consisting principally of African weapons. There were to be seen a collection of musical instruments of all descriptions, some so simple as to make one wonder how any symphony could be got out of them. A well-filled shelf, with a plain oak desk, littered with written matter, with some flowers here and there, about completed the outward circumstance of the room into which our visitor was ushered. Pushing well forward the only easy chair in the room, and placing his friend in it with a smile of welcome, he threw himself upon a low seat beside him, touched a bell on a side table, and ordered some refreshment.

" I hope you don't mind my old-world ways," remarked Kwamankra. " You know, though I have lived in this country fairly long, off and on, I like to sniff a bit of the African air somehow where'er I go."

" That is perfectly natural, at least with a well-balanced mind," correcting himself, said Whitely; " but what I can't understand is that you don't seem a bit Eastern in your methods of work. To judge from that pile yonder," eyeing the notes mischievously, " one wouldn't think you were over here for a holiday."

" Oh, that is only a bit of derivative work.

You have no idea how interesting it is. Would you like to see what I am doing? "

" How good of you! I should be delighted."

" I shall soon be finishing now," said Kwamankra excitedly. " You see I am at the letter ' Y.' And that reminds me : you remember a while ago my taking you to task over the feebleness of the idea of ' God ' in the Anglo-Saxon language. I have just got the corresponding word here in, *Fanti*. It is a big word, so big that you can hardly manage it :—

NYIAKROPON.

Does it convey any meaning to you? How can it? And yet, I can assure you, my friend, it is no mere barbarous jargon. It is the combination of distinct root ideas in one word. It relates back to the beginning of all things visible, and links the intelligent part of man with the great Intelligence of the universe. Breaking up the word into its component parts, as I have done, we have :—

> *Nyia nuku ara oye pon.* That is,
> *He who alone is great."*

" How very suggestive. Who should have thought it? " observed Whitely, enthusiastically.

" Well, let us take the next word, then,

NYAMI,

which is still more suggestive, and analyse it.
Broken up, it stands in bold relief thus :—

Nyia oye emi.   That is,
He who is Iam.

Now compare the Hebrew *Iam* hath sent me, and
you have it. Nor is this a fanciful play upon
roots, for our people sing unto this day :

' *Wana si onyi Nyami se?*
Dasayi wo ho inde, okina na onyi,
Nyami firi tsitsi kaisi odumankuma.'

meaning :

' *Who says he is equal with God?*
Man is to-day, to-morrow he is not,
Iam is from eternity to eternity.'

" You can now understand," continued Kwamankra in a low, sad tone, " why your difficulty
surprised me. But now that I come to think of it,
it may be due to the limitations of your language."

" After what you have just shown me, I must
confess there is a deal in what you say; and somehow you Orientals manage to keep your hold on
the eternal verities, where we flounder and are
lost."

" Pardon me, my good friend, not quite that. As
yet you are only drifting, drifting, drifting away

from the ancient moorings that you Westerners built in sand. Jesus Christ came from the East. In Bethlehem he was born, and in Egypt was he nurtured; and, yet, you seek to teach Him us. We have caught His Spirit and live; you follow the letter and are tossed hither and thither by every wind. Forgive me when I say that the future of the world is with the East. The nation that can, in the next century, show the greatest output of spiritual strength, that is the nation that shall lead the world, and as Buddha from Africa taught Asia, so may Africa again lead the way."

" I am not prepared to dispute the matter with you, Kwamankra, and there seems to be a good deal of truth in what you say; but how about the doubt deep down in my own heart? That is a personal affair, you know. In a word, what think you of the Christ? "

" What a clever dialectician you are, Whitely, to be sure? If I did not know you so well, I would hardly think you were serious. You throw back to me the question I put to you a while ago, and you lay upon me the burden of solving my own riddle."

Whitely's voice was low and sad with a suspicion of emotion in his whole manner, as he said : " Forgive me , Kwamankra, if I have seemed flippant; I was never more serious in my life. I

B

have arrived at a crisis in my career which may
mean disaster at any moment; and, what is more,
until this day I have never had the courage to
speak it out to any of my friends for fear they
would mock at my doubts.''

Kwamankra turned upon his friend a look full
of penetration and sympathy; and, for the
moment, Whitely felt uneasy under the searching
glance of the Eastern student. It seemed to him
as if in that instant Kwamankra had probed his
inner nature and found it shallow.

'' According to our ideas, Whitely, one broad
divinity runs through humanity, and whether we
are gods, or we are men, depends upon how far we
have given way to the divine influence operating
upon our humanity; and, comparing one system
with another, I must confess there was in the man
Christ Jesus a greater share of divinity than in
any teacher before or after Him, and that was in
my mind when I was wondering what Marcus
Aurelius had in common with Jesus Christ.''

'' But tell me, Whitely, supposing Jesus Christ
had been born of an Ethiopian woman instead of
Mary of the line of David, do you think it would
have made any difference in the way he influenced
mankind? ''

'' What a strange question,'' returned Whitely;
'' our Lord born of an Ethiopian woman? ''—

forgetting his doubts for the moment—" Whatever put such an idea into your head? I am sure
you are the first man who has given expression to
such a thought."

" Yes, it is strange "—and there was a vibra-
tion of the intensest pathos in Kwamankra's voice
—" that an African should venture to think that
the Holy One of God might have been born of his
race. I can easily interpret your thoughts; but,
tell me, what is there extraordinary in the idea? "

" Oh, I don't know. Habits of thought, con-
vention, and all that sort of thing, I suppose.
And yet I am hardly qualified to speak upon these
things," said Whitely, softening.

He rose to go. He was due farther west to see
his people. Before leaving, he laid a hand on
Kwamankra's shoulder, and looking gravely into
his face, he said : " It is a pity, Kwamankra, I
did not meet you a little earlier in my career.
But even now, it may not be too late. Good-bye!
Mind you meet me at Liverpool Street Station
before the hour for the night train up. Good-
bye! "

CHAPTER II.

SOWING THE WIND.

SILENCE prevailed in the room, except for the stitch, stitch, stitch, of a woman past the early bloom of womanhood who, at first stitching merely to pass away the time, now thrust the needle viciously into the embroidery, as if bent upon drawing some secret from the heart of the silken cords of life.

Presently she began to cry—hot burning tears which flowed from the passion of a heart which sought for rest and found none.

The curtains were down, and, save a glowing fire which a young student kept poking for no reason at all, the atmosphere of the room, as far as these two souls were concerned, was in strange keeping with the fog outside. They were man and wife, these two, at least before God. Of his own free will he had made love to her in far away Africa, and she had responded. But that was years ago. She, then, a buxom, lively lass, he an intelligent youth of the National University. She, now in England, only a nurse-maid; he a successful

student, equipped and ready to carry all the world
before him. Yes, they were man and wife, these
two; yet were they both ill at ease, and the young
man would have willingly trusted himself to the
tender mercies of the London fog. Yet he could
not go. It was the law of compensation. He
was fairly caught in his own meshes, and fate
called upon him to face the music.

To do Tandor-Kuma justice, for that was the
youth's name, he had always intended to remain
steadfast in his promise to Ekuba. But now the
circumstances were changed, and he was doing his
best to grapple with a most difficult situation.
How could he, a professional man, used to all the
luxuries of English life and habit, take back with
him to start a career in Africa a nurse-maid?
And what would he do, if asked to Government
house? Thoughts such as these passed through
his mind and made him obdurate to the pleading
of the woman at his feet.

"If you cry again, Ekuba, I shall leave you.
You know it is too bad when I am doing all my
best to amuse you in this horribly depressing
weather."

"Oh, you needn't trouble about that, Tandor-
Kuma. I know you will leave me in any event.
You don't think I have lived all these years
without knowing what you men are. You press

weak women into your service, and when you have won their sympathy, for a dream you toss them away like this," viciously kicking at the rug before the fire.

"Now, Ekuba, try and be reasonable. You mustn't think I am going to desert you. Bad as we men are, we have our ideals, and we never rest until we realise them."

"Good! That beats all the cant I have ever heard! What is the next, pray? And women have no ideals, of course! Uncultured women do not feel, do not think! They are just like clay in the hands of you men to mould—to make or mar."

"Now you are getting angry. Let us discuss this matter dispassionately."

Instead of that, Ekuba burst into a paroxysm of grief which Tandor-Kuma found it hard to control. By degrees, she grew calmer, and, sticking a pin or two in her head-gear, she snatched up her wraps and stood ready to depart.

"Tandor-Kuma," she said, "you have your ideals, and I have mine. Let us part like friends. I shall not give you the opportunity of dismissing me like a cur. Good-bye, for the present! It may be we shall meet again." And before the young student could frame a suitable answer, Ekuba was gone.

CHAPTER III.

LOVE AND LIFE.

1.

THE Mfantsipim National University had, about the time that these studies open, been already doing good work in Fanti-land. It had its origin in the national movement which swept over the country in the stormy days of 1897, when the people, as if moved by a sudden impulse, rallied round the Aborigines Society and successfully established the principle of land tenure under which the country has since thriven.

It had been felt for a long time by men of light and leading in Fanti-land that the salvation of the people depended upon education; that to educate the youths of the country properly depended upon trained teachers; and that it was the work of a university to provide such training ground.

The people did not wait for endowments from the rich and the philanthropic, or for money-making syndicates to start the work; but quickly collecting a few enthusiastic young men, these went about from province to province and from village to village trying to instil into the commonalty what the country lost by the neglect of education. The people began to understand and to talk about the matter in the wayside places. So that when Jubilee Day came round, and from province to province throughout all the states of Fanti-land the gong-gong of the *Amanhin* went round for contribution by the people to the National Educational Fund, great was the enthusiasm of high and low, and there was not a hamlet throughout the land which did not send its fair share of contribution. Even the children threw into the *Kruba* in the market places their three-penny-bits.

Among the enthusiastic band who canvassed the educational question was Kwamankra, and none more ardently than he. He was a man of remarkable intelligence, who, receiving the best education the schools of those days could afford, had, by hard work and natural taste for book-learning, so impressed the community with his ability that at the age of nineteen he had been entrusted with the editorship of the national news-paper, and had already come to be regarded as one of the coming leaders of the people.

Upon the opening of the National University,

Kwamankra gave up newspaper work and joined the University staff. He was foremost in bringing forward schemes to prevent the work of the University becoming a mere foreign imitation. He kept constantly before the Committee from the first the fact that no people could despise its own language, customs, and institutions and hope to avoid national death   For that reason the distinctive garb of students, male and female, was national with an adaptability suggestive of the advanced state of society.   It was recognised that the best part of the teaching must be done in the people's own language, and soon several text-books of known authority had, with the kind permission of authors and publishers, been translated into Fanti, thereby making the progress of the student rapid and sound.

The scheme involved, as it has been shown, the turning out of efficient teachers, and as the University was affiliated to that of London and in working correspondence with some of the best teaching institutions in Japan, England, Germany, and America, the work done was thorough. A young man or woman obtaining a certificate as a trained teacher was sure of work in any part of the country at a recognised salary.   Upon arriving in a province, all that the teacher would have to do would be to present his credentials to the

Secretary for Education of the *Omanhin*, who, having a list of districts ready for a teacher, would at once introduce the new-comer. Generally he would find a suitable school house with all necessary appliances, but not the children; and he would be given to understand by the Committee that whether the school house remained empty or filled depended upon his own energy and the interest he brought into his work, and, what was more, his rise to the maximum stipend would be the result of the maximum success expected. As a rule, the teachers were men who had their heart in their work, and the filling of the schools was a matter of two or three months.

The thirst for knowledge spread so rapidly that men and women took to attending night schools where they quickly picked up reading and writing in their own language, and such was the general eagerness for learning that translation work had become a distinct feature of the work of the University. Hence at the time that we made the acquaintance of Kwamankra, he was engaged upon derivative work in London. His health having given way somewhat as the result of excessively hard work, he had been recommended to go away for a bit, and taking advantage of the opportunity, he had visited Japan, Germany, and America to study their methods, winding up, as he planned out in his own mind, with a visit to England.

By this time the outlook of Kwamankra upon life was broadening; and the young man was beginning to cast in his mind the most useful avenue by which his life's work could be best accomplished. While he thought upon these things, that Divinity which shapes our ends, whether we understand or no, was shaping matters in a way for Kwamankra that he could hardly anticipate. By a resolution of the University authorities, while in London, an offer came to him to continue his stay for a period of three years certain, for the purpose of superintending the publications of several standard works in the vernacular that the University had arranged to bring out. When the offer came, he at once closed with it, seeing therein a way to the fixing of his future career. And so the die was cast. Having private means of his own, he joined the University of Cambridge, read jurisprudence for a year, and having then joined the Inner Temple, had, at the time that we met him along Tottenham Court Road in the company of Whitely, settled down in London to read law in grim earnest.

2.

In the far-away home in Africa, where

Kwamankra was born and bred, he had known a little orphan girl who attracted attention wherever she went by her simple, unaffected ways. She must have been under the ministration of some guardian angel, for if ever a person grew in favour with the gods and men, it was she. Daily she was to be seen in the temples of *Nanamu*, and no one was more attentive, or worried the old priest afterwards with such knotty questions. She was born well, and, having passed through a course in the University, was now visiting Europe for the first time to put the finishing touches to her education.

When Whitely parted with Kwamankra, the latter made his way to Holborn and wandered aimlessly down Oxford Street, his mind full of varied thoughts. He had always been a thinker, and this morning in his conversation with Whitely fresh avenues of thought had opened up in his mind which he wished to pursue undisturbed. As he watched the mighty procession of men, women, and children jostling one another, he was overwhelmed with a sense of the weariness which European civilisation had evolved for itself. But it was of the teaching of the Christian philosophy and its paradoxes that his mind was full. Was it not the Nazarene who said : " Come unto me all ye that are weary and heavy laden, and I will give

you rest "? Had he given this people, who professed to be his followers, rest in their constant
attempt to overreach one another, in the way they
trampled upon one another unto fame and
fortune? Again, he had called all his followers
brethren, and was not his the injunction to go
forth and teach all nations that all might be
brethren? And, even now, the words of Silas
Whitely, Divinity scholar of Queen's : " What a
strange question! Our Lord born of an Ethiopian
woman!"—again rang in his ears. What if
bishops, prelates, in the direct line of Him, Who
made Himself of no reputation, felt the same, and
yet dared to propagate his gospel among the
Ethiopian Gentiles? Were there to be paradoxes
all the way through? A religion which taught
one thing, and practised another, was it worth
following? And in his inmost heart he found
himself thanking the gods that he was a poor
benighted pagan according to the formula of the
Church.

In the frame of mind in which Kwamankra
was, he was in no temper to be disturbed; but as
luck would have it, he had not gone far when he
saw coming towards him a dark man, known
among his fellows as the Professor. He professed
all things, and knew nothing in particular. He
was in reality Kwow Ayensu, a student of several

years' standing at the Charing Cross Hospital, to whom, as far as one could judge, the question of a medical or a surgical diploma was of a secondary consideration. Kwamankra dodged the Professor, and made for the opposite pavement. The Professor as promptly crossed over, and familiarly tapping him on the shoulder, said in a gruff voice, " Hallo! old fellow, how are you? I have not seen you for quite an age; and what is the meaning of cutting an old chum like this, eh?"

Evidently there was no getting away from the Professor, and so Kwamankra resigned himself to his fate.

" The fact is," said Kwamankra, " if you want me to be frank with you, I wanted to be alone. I was so enjoying myself before you interrupted me. I love to observe without being observed."

" Do you include in your observations that of humanity in general?" dryly put in the Professor.

" Yes," replied Kwamankra. " To me it is the most interesting study, and the best theatre I find to be these very pavements, the performers being the moving throng of men and women. To study humanity in this guise is to me the acme of intellectual pastime, and much as I would like a chat with you another time, I am really sorry you disturbed me."

" Your case," said the Professor, " is a simple

one of cerebral contraction of the sympathies. Come with me, old boy, to the Argyle Rooms to-night, and I warrant you the finest study of humanity anywhere in London. You may notice without being noticed, and if you should feel inclined to thaw, by Jove! you will have your work cut out. Some of the latest arrivals are rare bits, and they are the rage of all the young hounds, misnamed men. Do come with me.''

'' I thank you for the kind invitation, but I am afraid I cannot come to the Argyle Rooms with you to-night, as I must catch the night train to Cambridge with a friend.''

'' Well, then, come with me to the York Hotel instead. It may be I shall be able to interest you, and, if you please, you may stand me a treat after. I hear some of you 'varsity chaps are very good that way. Your average rusty London student does not understand champagne suppers and that kind of thing.''

'' If it comes to that, Professor, we needn't go all the way to the York Hotel. We can just drop in at Slater's round the corner, and I will warrant you as good a lunch as you ever tasted. Come along now. I will take no refusal.''

It did not take much to persuade the Professor, and together they were soon seated at a well-appointed table in a comfortable corner. After lunch the Professor said to Kwamankra, "One good turn deserves another. I thought I would give you a bit of a surprise, but since the mountain would not come to Mahomet, I suppose he must go to it. The fact is, Mansa is in London, and is staying at the York Hotel with her father."

3.

When Kwamankra called at the hotel the next day to pay his respects he was surprised to learn that, an hour or so previously, Mansa and her father had taken the train for Harwich on their way to the Continent. The girl had always expressed a desire to see the principal countries of Europe, and as her father had a little business in the south of Germany, she had coaxed him, on the plea that it yet wanted a fortnight before she would be due to enter college, to take her with him. So pleased she was with her German surroundings, that when her father was returning to London, she was loth to come with him; and as she had always shown a decided inclination for music, it had been decided she should remain at school there for a year or two to pursue her studies.

Time passed and Kwamankra had no news of Mansa. All the Professor could tell him was that her father had returned to Africa, and the young lady was pursuing her studies on the Continent.

In the meanwhile, Kwamankra was quietly reading in the Temple. They were eventful years—those three short years in the heart of the metropolis. The science of jurisprudence had always attracted him. It opened to him vistas of justice and fair play between man and man, which strongly appealed to him. The influence of the stoical writings over the Roman jurists, producing a Law of Nations, showed him a way by which the nations of the earth, yielding to higher impulses, might mete out justice to the weak races of mankind. Moreover, the opportunity which it gave him of comparing the institutions and customs of his own country with other systems was an endless source of delight to him. Now was his opportunity to fit himself for the battle of life. He read, not for examinations, but for information. He drank freely from the vital springs of knowledge and found his soul satisfied. He could not help feeling that he had a call to duty, and that in the service of his race.

At the time of Kwamankra being called to the Bar he had invited to London for a day his friend Whitely. After the ceremony they repaired to the Haymarket to hear Mr. Beerbohm Tree in the part of Hamlet. As the curtain did not rise till 8.30, and the evening was particularly fine, they walked down to the theatre from the Temple, and the conversation naturally turned upon Shakespeare's masterpiece.

" You know, Kwamankra, I have never forgotten the conversation you and I had three winters ago along Tottenham Court Road, and I have been going deeply into the matter. I have been comparing the worship of Osiris by the Egyptians of your own race, the Akkadian philosophy, the religions of Zoroaster, of Buddha, and of Confucius, the teachings of the Greek mysteries, and of the stoic writings, and the farther I have gone into the matter the more puzzled I have become as to the right of the people calling themselves Christians to a monopoly of divine light. And as to the term ' heathen,' I think it arrogant for any devotee of any one sect to apply it to another. There is as much sense in it as the ancient Greeks dubbing all others barbarians. Here we are to-night, for instance, going to hear a play written by one William Shakespeare, a Christian gentleman, who flourished in the reign of Queen Elizabeth. I dare say if I stood in the pit of the Haymarket to-night, and made an open statement that William Shakespeare was a gentleman, but I had my doubts as to whether he was a Christian, I would be hooted down and hissed out of the theatre. Yet a superficial reading of some of his works will convince you that his senti ments, if he wrote from his inmost self, which he must have done, great poet as he was, were far from those of a Christian. See how Hamlet nurses in his bosom a feeling of revenge so poignant as to find satisfaction in killing the wicked king only at a moment when he will fall with all his sins upon his head. It reads like the work of a heathen, and yet I dare not suggest that William Shakespeare was a heathen at heart."

Kwamankra burst into a hearty laugh.

" Unless you have read Jevon to little purpose, you must admit that that argument is faulty. Yet I cannot help agreeing with you that the word ' heathen ' is a relative term, and perhaps your average Englishman has no right to call the average Ethiopian heathen. Ours was the cradle of civilisation, and that it had not the permanence that the Christian civilisation is likely to have does not make it any the less a civilisation; and I, for one, feel nothing but pity for the kind of ignorance which scoffs at what it does not understand."

The speaker stopped somewhat abruptly, and eyed the listener curiously. After a second, he continued :

" You know perfectly well, my good friend, that I am not a Christian. If not, what am I? Perhaps delicacy may forbid you saying what you think. But, believe me, I am not ashamed to be

called pagan, or heathen, or by any other such pet
word. With all due respect to St. Paul, we worship that we do know. The fact of the case is,
that from the days of the great teachers of Christianity you Christians have not taken the trouble
to understand any other system but your own."

" You know, Kwamankra, turning off the subject, I have taken my degree, and I am soon due
for ordination," said Whitely. " But all these
years the reason and the faith within me have been
in such deadly conflict as to leave my senses reeling.
Yet the die is cast; I have given my name in to the
Bishop; I cannot look back for fear of breaking my
mother's heart."

" I am sorry for you, my dear friend," said
Kwamankra, " but, perhaps, you don't look at the
matter from the broad point of view that an outsider can look at it. I know, of course, something
of the religions of the past. I have studied our
own Eastern systems and compared them with the
system you Westerns have adopted, and find that
one broad divinity as well as humanity runs
through them all. You will grant, I think, that
there was something that lifted man to God in all
the systems you have named, and in others of
which, as yet, you know nothing, and that some of
the founders of these systems, such as Epictetus,
Cleanthes, Buddha Gautama, were men whose

ideals of self-suppression and communion with
God were of no mean order. I am free to say that
there is a marked difference between them all and
the Christ, as much as there is a difference
between the stoical writings and the Gospel of St.
John. Jesus Christ was a living, breathing, God-
in-man personality, linking human son-ship with
divine fatherhood. Buddha Gautama, for example, never truly realised his own son-ship with
God as to reveal that relationship to man. He
strove to pierce the secret of the universe, but never
quite succeeded. Then as to reason and faith and
the load of doubt—well, if you ask me whether the
birth of Jesus Christ was a natural birth or a
supernatural one, as an outsider, all I can say is,
I don't know, nor does it matter one jot whether
it was the one or the other. Similarly, if you ask
me whether He did ascend into Heaven with His
bodily form, defying the law of gravitation, I say
I don't know, nor does it matter. But this I do
know, that His life and work and His interpreta-
tion of the ways of God with man may so draw
one to Him as brother, friend, master, and,
through Him, to God as Father, Almighty
Sovereign, Benefactor and Guide, and that should
be enough for the average man whose object is not
arrogantly to question high Heaven, but to make
his way thither humbly and piously.'²

When they arrived at the theatre the curtain was just up, and, for a moment, they were engrossed in the simple setting of the play for which Mr. Beerbohm Tree is so remarkable in his Shakespearean representations. In Scene III., where Polonius utters the precept : " Beware of entrance to a quarrel; but, being in, bear't that the opposed may beware of thee," Kwamankra, poking his friend in the rib, whispered, " That is Christian sentiment with a vengeance."

When the curtain next went up, Whitely drew the attention of Kwamankra to a bevy of dark girls with an elderly man, who seemed to be playing the part of chaperon, and who were soon joined by a couple of young men. Kwamankra followed the direction indicated by Whitely, and nearly jumped out of his seat with excitement.

" What is it, Kwamankra ? " asked Whitely. " You generally are so cool."

" Pardon me, but the fact is, I must introduce you at once. Those are my friends the Abans, and I am very much mistaken if the young lady at the corner is not Miss Mansa. Come along ! " And he literally dragged Whitely after him.

The old gentleman saw the twain coming in their direction, and beamed all over with delight. He was a good-hearted soul, and loved to see the sons of Ethiopia acquit themselves honourably in a strange land, and he had heard nothing but what was good of Kwamankra. The enthusiasm with which Kwamankra was greeted by his friends struck Whitely forcibly, and he did not at all notice the few seconds that passed before he was introduced.

During the interval, Mansa, who hated all crushes, preferred to remain where she was, so Kwamankra fetched her some refreshment, and stayed to talk to her.

" So you deserted us for the Continent without a moment's notice. It was really bad of you, and I hope you have made up your mind now to make full amends."

" Yes, I didn't like the life here," said Mansa. " Somehow it didn't suit me. Besides, I had no friends here, and as my father was going away, I felt I could not stay."

" You must have found Stuttgart congenial, to judge from the length of time you have been away. Your father has been telling me a little about it, and I hoped to hear more from you."

" Oh! that must be another time. See, the curtain is about to rise, and here come trooping in the Abans. You know we arrived only this afternoon by the Dover train, and met the Abans at the hotel; and as they were coming to see Hamlet, my father thought it would be nice for us to come with them."

" Now, that reminds me, by a stroke of ill-luck, I arrived at your hotel the day you left for the Continent half an hour too late, to find the bird had flown."

Mansa felt a little confused; and just then the curtain rose.

The rest of the play interested Kwamankra little, and he was not at all sorry when cheer after cheer called Mr. Tree over and over again before the footlights to receive such an ovation as few artists have received before or since.

"Mind you call before I leave for Africa," said the old gentleman, as Kwamankra and Whitely said good-night.

The friends talked little on their way back to the Temple, and Whitely, divining what was passing in his friend's mind, respected his silence. Before separating for the night, however, Whitely said, " Allow me, Kwamankra, to thank you for giving me such an agreeable evening in such a cultured company. Your friends, by Jove, are a credit to Africa, and it makes me feel inclined to lead a crusade against narrowness and prejudice."

" Thank you so much. I am glad you think so well of my friends. I hope you will sleep well after all the day's dissipation." This, as Kwamankra showed his friend to his room.

4.

For the next few weeks, Mansa and Kwamankra saw a good deal of one another. From the first, there was a congeniality between the two which went to make all intercourse natural, pleasant, and spontaneous. It was as if they had known one another all their lives; and it seemed the most natural thing that henceforth their joint lives should run in the same tenor. One day, as the twain sat chatting over an afternoon cup of tea, Mansa fetched a letter from a writing-table and, carelessly spreading it out, said :

" I forgot to tell you, when last you were here, that I have been offered the post of head-mistress of the junior classes of our home university. I am sure you will be delighted with the idea, for I am going to accept it, and my father agrees with me."

" How can you think of such a thing ? " burst out Kwamankra almost indignantly.

His manner was so sudden that Mansa could not possibly control herself.

" Now, what have I done to call for such sharp treatment ? " she demanded firmly, yet playfully.

" Forgive me, Mansa, if I have spoken with unwonted heat, only I was thinking—well, I was thinking you might teach me instead."

" What an absurd idea ! How can I teach such

a big, strapping fellow like you? " said Mansa. " Besides, you are so clever. Surely, you mock me."

" Believe me, my dear child," and there was a slight tremor in the manly voice, " I was never more in earnest in my life."

Mansa seemed puzzled. After a little hesitation, she said :

" You call me ' child,' and yet you would have me believe that I can teach you. Can you be serious ? "

" Yes, I am quite serious. ' And a little child shall lead them,' " he quoted. " I was hoping," pursued Kwamankra, " that yours would be the task to teach me the way of duty, and that, when found, you would help me to tread it."

" But how do I know what your duty is? Who can tell better than yourself ? Moreover, the gods of our fathers can teach you it, if you need guidance. Don't you know that, Kwamankra ? "

" Yes, I know that. But this also I do know, that the gods are wont to make use of human instruments in approaching men. The Infinite finds expression in the finite, and the ideal is realised in the actual. And it has often occurred to me that the child-like hand that shall guide me through life's labyrinthine ways is the self-same one that I now hold tenderly in my own."

She began to understand. She made an effort as if she would withdraw her hand. She hesitated, and the next moment she surrendered the other also.

"You will be my teacher, then?" asked Kwamankra, half-persuasively, half-triumphantly.

"Yes," she simply answered. "So may the gods of our race help me!"

As the days passed, the twain grew in that mutual understanding, the true basis of all happy unions. Now and again he would tell her of his prospects, which he laughingly said were nil, having inherited little else beyond a clear head and a willing heart for work, with which he hoped they would be able to forge their way in life together; to which Mansa would sweetly say that she wished she had a fortune to make things easy, but since she had it not, she would bring him the next best, a loyal heart and true, at which Kwamankra would chide her, and say that was the best of all.

Little by little, Mansa told Kwamankra all that had happened in her little life since the days he knew her as a child of ten.

"You know," she said, talking to him one day, "I often invoked *Nanamu* that I might be permitted to travel to see a little bit of the world, and it seemed they heard me; for soon after, my father

took it into his head to visit Europe with me after
1 had successfully passed my examinations at our
university. When we arrived here, the life of the
people seemed to me artificial. Perhaps I could
not have expressed my feeling then in those words,
but, anyhow, I felt as if I was not in my proper
element. Chance took me to Germany. I found
things very different there—there, in the Black
Forest, I got into direct touch with Nature; the
song of the birds, the bleating of the lambs, the
fragrance of the fields, all seemed so natural, and
I said to myself : Here is my proper place; here
the atmosphere wherein my nature may expand.
The rest you know. And now, what think you of
the result ? ''

For answer, Kwamankra caressingly drew her
nearer to his side.

Summer was waning into autumn, and the
chrysanthemum and the sweet mignonette were in
bloom, when the lovers decided upon marriage
before returning to Africa, where Kwamankra
was to start a practice. It was to be a simple
affair, at which there were to be no bride's-maids
or groom's-men, and only the nearest friends were
to be asked. Mansa appeared in church on the
wedding-day in a simple African costume of her
own design, tastefully got up, and when someone
asked her the reason for her choice, she said she

knew it would please her husband, and, besides, it answered best to her own conception of what was proper. And, " so, these were wed," to employ ,Tennyson's words.

Kwamankra was not long in taking up the duties of life in grim earnest with his dear little wife to cheer and to comfort him. From the first success smiled upon them, either as the result of honest, strenuous effort, coupled with natural ability, or as a mark of the favour of the gods, or both. Gradually they built up a big practice, and by the time their little boy was able to toddle from room to room, and call "Fadder! Mudder!" they had a sweet little home of their own, with plenty of flowers, and sunshine, and love, and God's blessing. Five short, very short, happy years of mutual love and association, and then there came a cloud which, for the moment, seemed to Kwamankra's breaking heart and tearful eyes without the silver lining; for, with the advent of their second born, a sweet baby girl, Mansa, poor wife and mother, paid with her life for that of her child, who, as though she could not stand the gloom she had brought to this once bright home, soon joined her mother, and made the former gloom twice gloomier, and father and son were alone with a twice two-fold bond of love between their souls and the souls of those that had gone before.

And when his little boy of three asked Kwa-mankra : " Where is ' Mudder ? ' " or " ‚Where is Sissie ? " he would say : " ' Mudder ' is gone to God, or Sissie is gone to God," as the case might be, and would turn aside his face, lest his little one might know the full extent of their woe.

CHAPTER IV.

LOVE AND DEATH.

" 'Fadder,' when I was in Heaven, I couldn't come to you; but I could go to ' Mudder.' I was with ' Mudder ' in Heaven."

" But why couldn't you come to me ? " She hesitated.

" See, ' Fadder,' I have put the pin through," holding up a match-box triumphantly. Then, presently, in baby fashion, taking up the idea—" I was a big girl in Heaven."

" So you were, darling," and he bent down and kissed her tenderly.

*   *   *   *

" Where the bird warbles earliest, and new light
.Wakes the first buds of spring; where breezes sleep
Or sigh with pity half the summer night,
While the pale, loving stars look down to weep.
There lies our grave; a slender plot of ground,
'Tis all of earth we own; no cross, no tree,
Nothing to mark it, but a little mound;
But there my darling stays; she waits for me,
The lily in her hand; and when I come,
She will be glad to greet me, and will say,
' Your lily, dearest, gives you welcome home,'
But oh! dear Lord, I hunger with delay;
Tell me, blest Lord, shall I have long to wait?
For I must haste, or she will think me late."

CHAPTER IV.

LOVE AND DEATH.

1.

The newborn child opened her eyes upon a mysterious world. In her little face was a puzzled look—a look of half doubt and half knowledge. There was one who seemed to understand the meaning of this doubting expression, and that was the father of the child.

She had come in answer to prayer—in response to the call, long, earnest and pure of motive from mortal to a god, which the gods are wont to answer. Not that the father of the newborn child did not believe in God; but he was sure that in the hierarchy of the heavens, there was order and rule, and, even as the master-mind controlled subordinate intelligences, making them to do and to will of his good pleasure, so did the Father of all, call him *Nyiakropon, Zeus, Ra, Jupiter*, or by what name soever you please, control the powers and dominions of other spheres and the agencies of this world.

And so it had come to pass that for full twenty changes of the moon he had prayed fervently to the God of Love to visit him in his loneliness, and this child had come in response to that prayer.

D

But he had also prayed for light, for he knew, according to the teaching of *Nanamu*, the priests and prophets of his tribe, that Love and Light dwelt together in the highest heaven.

2.

To him who saw this vision, the idea of death was familiar. Among his people, at break of day, as men passed one another in the market-places, they would greet one another and say, "*Akioo*," meaning, hail friend, thou yet livest. And if a man slept and woke no more, they would say he is gone to *Nanamu-Krome*, and, if he had been a good man, his friends would make libation to him, claiming his protection and guardianship in the ordinary affairs of life.

He had been a father once before—the happy husband of a happy wife in a home where love dwelt; and when death first took the wife and then the new-born babe, he left darkness behind where first was light. It all looked so strange. He only half realised it in the first flush of his sorrow. But as the days wore on, and the old familiar chair by the hearth remained vacant, the darkness in his heart seemed to deepen.

Gradually the light of understanding dawned upon his soul. He came to know that the spiritual side of love was of far greater value than all else beside, and read a spiritual meaning into the offices of love. Sorrow was the path that led him to the inncrmost shrine where he met God, the *Nyiakropon* of his race, and understood. He could stand by the open grave of his beloved— open, because by spiritual sympathy he could see her as she was—and say : '' I kiss these flowers ere I lay them on thy bosom; and when I say ' I,' I do not mean this frail body of mine, which is but a casket. Hear me, beloved ! I mean the soul in me, that which can have and has communion with thee, soul with soul, and spirit with spirit, how it does not matter. See, I throw thee a spiritual kiss, and I know thou returnest kiss for kiss, even as of yore.'' Yes, he had touched the depths of human happiness and the depths of human sorrow, and had come to know that the way to God led from the one to the other.

3.

The physical strain had been too much for Kwamankra. A lurking disease had begun to show dangerous symptoms. A hurried consultation had resulted in the doctors deciding upon an operation. He received the news with wonderful calmness. He rejoiced secretly in the prospect of the unconscious condition of the senses through which he would pass, and hoped against hope that

the intelligence of his nature, freed from earthly
trammels, might be free to concentrate themselves
upon things spiritual, and given a glimpse of the
city of the ancient dead of his race, where he was
sure his beloved dwelt. It was a wish born of
sincere anticipation which flew on the wings of
prayer to the Father of Spirits. As he passed off,
he was heard to murmur softly the name of his
wife, but none knew that, like Jacob of the
Hebrews, he had wrestled with God and prevailed.

In another sphere, as if from a dream, Kwamankra awoke, and, though he possessed not his
physical body, as it seemed to him, he was sure of
his identity as ever he had been. He commanded
the full use of his intelligence, and the scene
around him, though weird, was by no means un-
familiar. He had the feeling of one who, travelling to a far distant country, and, for the nonce,
forgetting the physical aspects of his native land,
upon returning, in a moment, recalls the old place
again. But it was not without misgiving, as he
gradually took in the scene around. It was at the
outskirts of the city, not built by men, that he found
himself. For walls the city was surrounded by a
great lake whose water was as clear as crystal, to
attempt to cross which were madness for a mortal
without aid.

As Kwamankra stood doubting within himself
what he should do, and deploring the presumption

which made him wish to encompass knowledge not
destined for man, suddenly there appeared before
him a being of such untoward mien that he was
anxious to fly from his presence, if he only knew
how. It had the aspect of a human being, but so
distorted were the features, and so woebegone the
expression, that he looked to all appearances half
man and half beast. Finding no possible way of
escape, Kwamankra took courage, and thus
addressed himself to the monster : " Sir, I am a
mortal from the nether sphere, which men call the
earth, and, unbidden, I have sought to catch a
glimpse of this glorious city which now I find it
were death for mortal to enter unaided. Pardon
my presumption, but tell me how I may gain entrance into yonder city, where I may find her
whom my soul loveth."

" Thou hast well spoken in that thou hast
mentioned the word ' love.' If truly thou art
moved by love, then art thou not far from thy
quest; and since thou hast uttered the password, I
will tell thee the way, which lies in simple trust.
Hear me and understand. I was a mortal like
unto thyself. I was ambitious and arrogant. I
hoped to scale high heaven by knowledge and by
the work of man's imagination. I tried and
failed, and I am what I am. The gods, in anger,
bade me stay here and point to mortals the way to
the city beyond, which I may not enter for full

thousand summers, as thou measurest time, until
my iniquity be purged.''

'' I do not understand thy speech,'' said Kwamankra. '' If thou art minded to help me, tell me
simply how I may cross over the lake, and win my
way to the glorious avenues beyond ? ''

'' Did I not tell thee that the way lies in mere
trust ? I have very little to add. Examine thine
own heart, and if there is aught in it that is not
sincere and true, thou mayest not enter in.''

Then, suddenly, Kwamankra bethought him how
in the temples of his native land, he was wont to
bow the knee to the God of Love. So, all else forgetting, bending the full force of his will to the
task, even on the banks of this impassable lake, he
knelt in fervent prayer that he might have
courage to cross over. And as he prayed he
seemed to enter into a trance, gradually losing consciousness of his immediate surroundings. When
he awoke there stood before him a beautiful youth,
clothed in a raiment of the fineness of gossamer,
which fell in graceful folds about his person. His
feet were encased in sandals of crystaline trans-
parency, and his head encircled with a chaplet of
lilies of the valley.

Kwamankra was about to speak, but the vision
raised his forefinger to his lips in token of silence,
and then in a voice full of pathos and sympathy
said, '' Mortal ! thy prayer to the God of Love and

Light hath been heard, and thy homage of love and trust met with favour, and I am bidden to lead thee across into yonder beautiful city; but, remember thou, that it is only so long as thy courage doth not fail, that thou canst safely cross over, that being the bridge over which mortals may enter. But fear not; thy love hath broken asunder the gates of death, and none may bar thy progress.''

Thus listening, Kwamankra suddenly found himself walking on the face of the crystal lake, and his companion with him. And when his heart began to fail him, he thought of his beloved, and took courage. Now and again he would seem to be sinking, only to rise again buoyant on the wings of confidence renewed; and soon the crystal lake was passed. There the vision left him, telling him his mission was ended, and he wot not what to do.

4.

While in this state of uncertainty, Kwamankra heard distant echoes of children's voices, so melodious was the strain, and, in harmony, far beyond aught he had ever heard. He strained his senses to hear more, and as the voices drew nearer, he was seized with a sudden wish to behold the beings from whom those sweet cadences proceeded. And that he might see unseen, he hid himself amidst

the flowers which grew in rich profusion outside
the city walls.

He had hardly done so, when lo! there came
trooping past a procession of young children, with'
palms in their hands, which they waved aloft, as
they sang, and the burden of their song was :
"Come, let us go to the Father's house; this day
he bringeth his children joy; the sun of salvation
is setting fast." So sweetly simple were these
children, and the only thing striking about them
was the purity of their countenances and the lofty
grace with which they carried themselves. Kwamankra greatly wondered when he recalled to
mind the angelic presence which had a while ago
left him. As the procession neared the city, the
company seemed to break into little groups, and
to disperse in different directions. They played
and gambolled and made fun, and, in all, there was
nothing fantastic or weird—so intensely human
were these children of the air.

In the meanwhile, the keeper of the gate had
hied him into the city, even to that part thereof
which faces the rising sun, where a goddess dwelt.
Thus the keeper of the gate addressed her, bowing
low : " Honoured among women! I am bidden
by *Nyiakropon*, the father of the gods, to bring
thee news of the coming of a mortal into the holy
city of *Nanamu*. Since thou art a goddess, thou
must know that since thy translation from nether

earth, he whom thy woman's heart prizeth above
all honour and glory hath constantly set himself
to purifying his heart and his ways, if haply he
may find the way to thee; and since he is faithful,
the constant desire of his heart, forced on the
breath of fervent supplications, hath pierced the
heaven of heavens and reached the ears of
Nyiakropon, wherefore it hath been decreed that
thou, honoured among women, should be the first
goddess in *Nanamu-Krome* to receive a mortal who
hath won his way to the holy gates. Arise, shake
off thy grief, and prepare to receive him whom
thy soul loveth.''

Him gratefully hearing, the goddess Mansa
arose, and commanded the maidens to get all
things ready, so that her coming Lord might not
feel strange in the city of the immortals. And
with music and with frolic did Katsina, her
little daughter, superintend all. As for Mansa
herself, to the house of praise did she proceed, and,
out of the fullness of her heart, did give thanks to
Nyiakropon. Before the holy altar she knelt, and
raising her heart in thanksgiving, the emotion of
her heart so overcame her, that she wot not how
to begin, or how to end her thanksgiving.

And wherefore was the goddess moved, and
whence the emotion of her heart! Scarcely could
she veil from memory an earthly scene of un-
paralleled pathos and solemnity, as the hour of

parting came. It was the last day of the fever
which burnt out her earthly life. There, in the
old familiar chamber, in the home where dwelt
love and light and all that she then, untutored,
prized dearest in heaven or on earth, stood husband and child—their first born, bone of their
bone, flesh of their flesh, so full of promise. She
knew her hour had come, and she must needs die,
and her little woman's heart rebelled against the
decree of the gods. An inward struggle seemed
to be going on within her at that critical moment.
At last she was heard to ejaculate : " Oh, God,
see where stand my husband and my child. I
cannot bear to see their grief-stricken faces. If
it be Thy will, spare me to them. But, if not,
not as I will, but as it seemeth good to Thee."
It was a bitter struggle—this struggle of the heart—
if haply it might secure its dearest wish against
the decree of heaven. But she was sincere in
giving *Nyiakropon* the choice. She had fought
and won, and the highest heaven had sealed the
victory. Thus the passing away of Mansa. As
for Kwamankra, hope ever more sprang up youthful in his heart. Over and over again he found
himself wondering whether his beloved was truly
dead, or dead only to his physical senses. And,
confidence renewed, evermore building upon
adamantine foundations, wafted a vow to heaven
that his one quest would be to learn the way to
her.

5.

" Katsina, mine," said the Goddess Mansa, " I want you to attend to what I am about to say. Ever since you came to me in answer to my tender call, I have taught you that but a thin veil divides *Nanamu-Krome* from the nether world where thy father and brother dwell, and that the veil is drawn, whenever it pleaseth heaven, for converse between immortals and men. This day shalt thou see thy father, for, even now, he is within the city walls at the main gate. Go, bid him welcome to *Nanamu-Krome*, for I may not go to him yet. Joyously did the maiden saunter forth to do her mother's behest, and, even at the main gate, as she had been forewarned, she met her father to whom she said, " Hail, father ! Mother hath sent me to welcome thee home." At this Kwamankra was startled beyond measure, but, not wishing to betray his bewilderment, he said, " I do not understand, little maid; pray, who may thy mother be, and how knew she that I was here ? "

" Do you not know me, father ? " said the damsel, half reproachfully. " Mother told me you were coming, and so I ran to meet thee; but how she knew you were here she did not tell me. But, you know, mother is a goddess, and she knows a good many things." The saying surprised Kwamankra, and he turned it over in his mind what it might mean. Was it possible that the devotion and the trust and the love of his girl-wife had blossomed into a personality which was half god and half human even in the nether world? The case of his little girl was easy to understand, for he had caught the import of the words of the poet who wrote :

"Day after day we think of what she is doing
    In those bright realms of air;
  Year after year, her tender steps pursuing,
    Behold her grown more fair."

Yes, she was fairer than the lilies, brighter than the sunbeams, purer than snow-flakes—his own little Katsina in this realm of light, and yet he had prayed for her return. For a moment he was lost in thought, then suddenly turning to his little girl, he embraced her with all the warmth of a father's heart, and eager to learn all he might of his girl-wife, he said, " Tell me, dear, what may a goddess be like?"

" How funny, father, what am I like? Have I not hands and feet and lips to return kiss for kiss?" And suiting the action to her words, she covered the bent face of Kwamankra with kisses. Even as the home-sick traveller, returning to his native shore, suddenly recalls distant echoes of the past, so did Kwamankra begin to catch

glimpses and to recall impressions of the sacred
abodes of *Nanamu-Krome*. It seemed to him, as
if in some bygone age from this self-same abode
of the ancient dead, the gods had sent him on an
errand to mortals. Even as he thought, the
impression deepened in his mind, that one day
the gods had said to him : " Kwamankra, this day
we send thee forth into the nether sphere to be
for us a witness unto the truth; for mortals are
ever wont to go away from the truth, whereupon
we gods are ready to destroy them. Go, as a
thinker among the thoughtless, convince them of
their error, proclaim unto them the sovereignty
of truth and the eternal majesty of *Nyiakrapon*,
the god of truth." It seemed to him that in
obedience to this call, he had gone forth, full of
courage, full of zeal, resolved to obey the command
of the gods; and lo! before his work was half
done, here he was, as it were in a dream, back to
Nanamu-Krome. He shuddered as he thought
upon these things, and greatly feared lest he had
stirred up the anger of the gods against himself
by leaving undone his duty. What would he have
to say to his wife upon meeting her this very day !

Meanwhile, his little daughter poured into his
ear, child-like fashion, the story of the abodes of
the ancient dead. But with all her childish ways,
there was something remarkable in the way she
put things. A turn or two soon took them to the

principal highway of the city of the immortals;
and here there burst upon his view a scene which
filled him with awe and curiosity. It was simple,
yet majestic, ethereal yet earthly; and one feeling
uppermost in him was that he had seen the like
before in some forgotten age. For a busy, noisy
thoroughfare with a multitude of men hurrying
hither and thither, here were, as it seemed, a
number of peaceful avenues, wearing a beautiful
green, like unto moss, which met in one grand
broadway. Each avenue was edged with luxuriant
shrubs and plants whose leaves showed the most
delicate tints of the rainbow in beautiful blend.
Here and there lifted their sinewy arms giants of
the forest not unlike the cedars of Lebanon. The
different walks seemed designed with an eye to
quiet contemplation. Now and again the avenues
ended abruptly in an ingeniously laid-out garden
from which again avenues continued to the
broadway. Here and there burst into view magnifi-
cent temples. The temples, as Katsina took pains
to explain to her father, had been raised by
immortal hands, not for prayer, but for praise.
A service of praise was just ending, as the twain
arrived at the portals of a beautiful temple, and
presently the avenues teemed with a moving
throng, but with all the congregation, there was
neither hurry nor bustle. The men were robed in
a kind of loose garment over which was thrown

in graceful folds across the left shoulder a
raiment of the softest material, crimson in colour.
They wore sandals on their feet and garlands of
red roses and lilies intertwined around their
heads. The crimson shade of their apparels
showed that they had passed through the narrow
gate of sacrifice; the roses in their chaplets were
for a token that over the bridge of sorrow they had
passed into the joy of *Nanamu-Kromo*; and as for
the lilies they merely pointed to the truth that
humility becometh well the triumphant. Sandals
they wore, because they had borne the heat and
the burden of the day, for full oft in the Sahara
of life they had had occasion to cry :—

> *Ekwan yi owari, Nyiakrapon*
> *Whe bra ma ahedzi yina atsitsiwu,*
> *Na minan aprepra, mutu ontu!*
> *Naasu wuada na mayi da wayim,*
> *Ga'm Kwan, Nyiakrapon!*

meaning :

> The way is long, Nyiakrapon,
> Behold the torn and scattered garment,
> And the bleeding feet that can scarce move on!
> Yet to thee only I may look.
> Oh! guide me Nyiakrapon!

One thing struck Kwamankra, and it was this :
the teeming multitudes represented every kindred,
race, people, and nation under the sun. It was
a congregation of select souls, men and women who

had humbly done their duty, and done it well, in another life. That was all.

6.

By now the mansion of the Goddess Mansa was within view, and Kwamankra could faintly decipher certain words writ large on the portals. The characters scintillated as if done in living fire; but, upon nearer approach, he noticed that the effect was produced by the silvery beams of a moon-like orb which, by day and by night, gave life and light to the abode of the gods. Thus Kwamankra read :

> " Lead thou me on, *Nyami*,
> And thou, O Destiny,
> Whithersoever thou ordainest,
> Unflinching will I follow;
> But if from willing heart
> I will it not,
> Still must I follow ! "

He read and pondered, and the more he thought of them, the more he wondered why they were written over the portals of Mansa's place. And while Katsina ever and anon impressed a point, bidding her father note this or that particular temple, even while she was yet warm in her account, they had arrived at the outer court of the mansion, and, saying, " There is mother come to meet us," with a cry of joy and a run, she was in her mother's arms.

"Katsina mine, run into the inner court and quickly set fruit and wine for thy father, for he must be weary after a long journey." So saying, she slipped past the child, and, in a moment, husband and wife were locked in a happy embrace; but even as the panting heart, after long waiting, at last receiving that which it had yearned for, breaks down and cries aloud for joy, so did the twain sob on one another's neck.

"Come, 'tis not seemly for us to give way like this when the gods have been so kind to us, nor must a goddess show weakness in many tears."

"I forget; Katsina told me so," said Kwamankra, starting back.

"How silly of you," said Mansa, "look at me, is there any difference between what I was and what I am, or can aught that may befall thee or me in time or eternity, save neglecting the will of the gods, make me less thy captive, thy bond maiden?"

"'Tis well said. But since thou inquirest, I must own that I see in thee a grandeur of soul, a depth of emotion, that mere mortals do not possess. Yet could I spot thee out among a thousand women. Tell me, art thou in very truth a goddess?"

"Yes, I am a goddess; for *Love* is of *God*, and

E

God is *Love.* And so art thou a god, only thy warfare is not yet accomplished. And to this intent was thy prayer heard, and leave accorded thee to visit this sacred abode, that thou mightest carry hence a knowledge which will aid thee in thy work."

" I can understand you being a goddess, but, surely, you mock me when you suggest that I am a god. Call me a thinker, a teacher, call me anything that is of the earth, but a god I cannot think that I am one, or can ever be."

A look of pain passed o'er the countenance of Mansa as in subdued tones she said : " It is even as it was revealed unto me. Yet another æon must pass over thy head before thou comest to thine own, before thou enablest me to add the finishing touches to thy habitation. All these years I have waited for the fruits of my suggestions, as thy guardian angel, and though thou hast learnt much, yet hast thou more to learn, even the lesson of simple trust. A little more doubting on thy part, and thou mightest have lost the chance of seeing my face this day. Yet how my woman's heart hath longed for thee—for a full and a lasting reunion."

" Pardon me, beloved, you talk of trust and seem to sorrow for my want of it. Believe me, I shall learn to trust more. But as for a habitation for me in this city, it is more than I can understand. Have pity on my simplicity, for I am but a mortal."

" I talk of naught, husband mine, that a mortal may not understand. Ever since my translation, I have watched over thee, even as a mother hen watches over her brood. Oft might'st thou have faltered, but that I prayed for thee, and my prayer was heard. Scarcely dost thou rise to the level of thy opportunities. Though a mortal, thou art a thinker, and, even among gods, none may rank higher. By knowledge God planned out the heavens, and laid deep the foundations of the earth. Only thou allowest full oft cold reason to usurp the place of simple trust, and in this thou art harder to learn than a little child. Now, hearken, unless thou becomest as simple and as trusting, æon after æon shall pass o'er thy head before our final reunion."

" It grieveth me to think, dear one, that the time for reunion is with me, and yet I command it not; but think not 'tis willingly done. Tell me, do you mean trust in little things as well as in great, in temporal matters as in matters of higher moment?"

" Yes, my beloved, light beginneth to dawn upon thy soul. Simple trust, remember, honoureth *Nyiakrapon*. Listen! When thou returnest to earth, opportunity will be given thee of preparing in this school, and oh! may'st thou be apt to learn.

E 2

For our beings must be rounded off, and every phase of our development completed, before translation. And for this purpose are we given opportunity after opportunity until the work of pruning be accomplished. It is all but the finishing touches that are required to thy habitation. Each mortal buildeth for himself a habitation in this sacred place. Some build of stone; some of stubble; unhappy they who raise their hopes upon the shifting sand.''

'' Yet thou speakest of the finishing touches being put by thee to that which is of my own building. Guardian angel mine, explain! ''

'' Truly, it is of thine own building. No one may build for another. Even love, such as mine, is helpless in such a case. Come with me, and I will show thee the structure that thou are raising for thyself.''

Kwamankra followed, greatly wondering what the full meaning of Mansa's words might be. Close to the mansion of the goddess was rising up a new structure of considerable beauty and strength before which Mansa paused lingeringly.

'' Behold,'' she said, '' the symmetry of this building. It is such as displeases not the gods. Yet, if thou perceivest clearly, thou wilt see a seam here, a fissure there, unevenness in places where there should be uniformity. Much as I love you, beloved, I cannot be unmindful of thy, imperfections. Reunion may not take place till thou hast laid the apex to a character, fit for a god to dwell in.''

'' Once more I fail to understand. How can my character form a dwelling place for a god? ''

'' ' Ye shall be as gods, knowing good and evil,' '' quoted Mansa, with sweet emphasis, more to herself than to her husband. Then fixing on him a look of tenderest sympathy, she said, '' In the beginning evil and good were created, and to man was given the command to rule and subdue the evil, and to foster and cause the good to prevail. That is the final reason of human experience, and man becomes a god when he has won the victory. It consists in the building of character, and one star may differ from another star in glory. When mortality fails, the immortal in man prevails and finds its home here where, in the cycle of the heavens, in the case of great souls, it becomes a god dwelling in the temple which character hath fashioned. The temple hath truth for foundation, love for superstructure, and child-like 'trust for apex. Do you now understand, beloved? ''

'' Yes, guardian angel mine.''

'' For encouragement,'' continued she, '' beholdest thou yonder rising tower in the structure which thou art raising for thyself whose pinnacle shimmers in the light of heaven? '' Kwamankra bowed assent. '' That is courage,'' said the goddess. "It stands somewhat prominently in the edifice, as thou canst see."

"But you puzzle me," said Kwamankra. "I have little courage, as men think of it and preach it. I love not the strife of mortals, neither do I excel in deeds of valour nor of strength wherein, as I understand, the gods delight. I have done no heroic deed in my time that I know of. I have won no battles, led no squadrons triumphantly against the hosts of men."

"Enough," broke in the goddess, with a slight gesture of impatience. "I know you have done none of these things. But wotest thou not as yet that I speak not of earthly things, and that, therefore, earthly comparisons are worthless? To love strife, to excel in deeds of nerve, to be leader in campaigns of slaughter — none of these is accounted great or courageous by the Father of the Gods. But to love truth, and to serve under its banner, come what may, that is courage truly, which will endure and stand the test of endless ages." Then turning upon him a look of intensest scrutiny and deepest sympathy, she continued: "Behold, you will stand before kings and princes and mighty ones of the earth to testify against corruption and wrong in high places in the name of truth. Thou hast courage, and the stars in their courses shall aid thee. And now take this message to the sons of men, and I give it thee as an emissary of the gods. Say unto the mighty that the cry of the afflicted and the distressed among the sons of Ethiopia has come up to us, and we will visit the earth. For gold the oppressor will find tinsel, and for precious stone adamantine rock which will fall upon the tinsel and grind it to dust, and the wind will scatter that which is ground unto the four corners of the earth, and men shall see it and wonder at the work of the gods. Lo! *Nyiakrapon* will establish in Ethiopia a kingdom which is different from all other kingdoms. Mammon will have no place therein, and an angel of light, with a two-edged sword, shall guard the gates thereof."

*   *   *   *   *

" And in order that thou mightest not falter by the way, when thou returnest to the earth, go to the city beautiful, the mother of the world, unto the part that faceth the setting sun, and thou shalt find a vestal virgin whose altar of love it hath been ordained should be lighted up by thee in incense to the God of Love. Go, she is true; thou hast my leave, and fare thee well! "

" But "—Kwamankra began.

" I know what thou would'st say," put in the goddess. " To obey is our present duty; and remember simple child-like trust is the apex of all—for thee as well as for me. It may be I shall come to thee, if need shall arise. So long as we trust, it

will all come right. Go, and again, fare thee
well!" And, as an anxious father, watching by
the side of a dying wife, restrains the anguish of
his heart, lest his little ones might know the full
meaning of their woe, even so did Mansa restrain
the anguish of her soul before her husband.

* * * * *

"Father, mother says I am to come back to thee
in the other world. I wonder if you will know
me when I come?" Kwamankra's eyes filled with
tears.

"Yes, I will, darling," he simply said.

* * * * *

When Kwamankra awoke, the work-a-day
world was going on in its accustomed way, and
the old earth still revolved upon its axis in the same
duration of time. And the sunlight chased the
shadows, and the shadows chased the sunlight, and
there seemed to be strife in the elements, but not
the strife of mortals. It was effort co-ordinating
with effort, and *Nyiakrapon* ruled over all.

* * * * *

The new-born child opened her eyes upon a
mysterious world. In her face was a puzzled
look—a look of half doubt and half knowledge.
After a few playful years she flitted away. Men
talked of a ripe soul. There was one who understood, but said nothing, and that was the father
of the child.

CHAPTER V.

IN THE METROPOLIS OF THE GOLD COAST.

In the year of grace, 1904, there was no such thing as a water supply in the town of Sekondi, the pet little preserve of His Majesty's Gold Coast Government. Nor was this in any way strange. The Government and the people of the Gold Coast had always depended upon Providence for such a common necessary of life as water. So, it happened, that when the Metropolis was being laid out into " High Streets " and open spaces, it had not dawned upon the authorities that man was a thirsty animal, and this notwithstanding gentle reminders on the part of experienced men in the past. If you search the Colonial archives, you will find that in the eighties of the old century Dr. Lamprey of the Army Medical Service proposed a simple scheme for supplying the ancient town of Cape Coast with fresh water. The Government went to sleep over the proposal, nor did it wake up over the suggestion to lead the waters of Homo to Accra, the headquarters of the Government. As matters stand, when Providence fails the Metropolis, men are known actually to resort to soda water for the daily ablution.

Now, if you want to see Sekondi at its best and the water question at its worst, you must approach the town in the month of March on one of Messrs. Elder Dempster's boats, at the season of the year, that is to say, when other parts of the country are already being bathed in refreshing showers. As you round off Tacradi Bay, you see the mother of Gold Coast civilisation enveloped in a sheet of overhanging clouds charged with electricity. The side view that is presented shows a city of great promise. Already there are signs of the heavens giving way, and raindrops patter on the ship's deck. But even while you are wondering what a wet landing you are going to have, a blaze of light breaks out on the north-east, and the Titan of the upper sphere leaps forth triumphantly over thunder and storm. As you divest yourself of your mackintosh, a cynical old coaster says to you : " That's Sekondi all over; I shouldn't be surprised if the tanks are all dry."

In other parts of the world harbour works generally precede railways; but here an apology for a pier-head does service for harbour accommodation. The result is you have to land in an open boat often with an angry surf surging around you. Let us assume, however, that you have landed safely. If you had known Sekondi in the

days of its pristine innocence, you will find that
an iron bridge now spans the ancient natural
boundary between the English and the Dutch
towns.   From the echoes beneath proceeds forth
the monotonous dirge of an asthmatic engine which
appears to be trying to do the work of two engines
in a climate which, according to some, is bad for
man, beast, and locomotive.

Where once stood the English town and the
uplands beyond, one can see at sunset a number of
well-arranged wooden houses on brick pillars,
looking quaint and striking in the distance, but
disappointing upon nearer view.   At the foot of
the hill lies the railway station, the first sign of
civilisation, as you meet it on the Gold Coast.   It
is the terminus of the '' Great North Western ''
of the Gold Coast.   And a beautiful line it is with
its sprightly curves and gradients and its thirty-
nine miles in something like three hours.   But I
am anticipating.

If you are not in a hurry to descend, you may
come with me to the Manager's bungalow, from
the spacious verandah of which you can catch a
bird's-eye view of Sekondi, bathed in the twilight,
as the sun moves leisurely in the western sky right
into the bosom of the mighty ocean.   So restful is
the scene !

If you know the history of this town, a
momentary sweep of the eye will bring back to

memory signs of a former strife; for overlooking
the Bay, there stands the old Fort, a symbol of
the strife between the Dutch and the English in
pre-locomotive days.   The struggle, in name, was
between two European nations, in reality between
two aboriginal factions, who, for aught one knows
to the contrary, might have otherwise lived in
peace.   The Dutch or the English flag was the
standard which drew the natives in thousands into
opposing camps, and for which they shed their
blood freely, only that the white man might obtain
freer scope to barter spurious drinks for the precious metal which the torrential rains washed to
the very doors of the aborigines.

It is a sad reflection, but a legitimate one, that
in the present day the successors of the leaders,
who bore the heat and the burden of the day in
order that British commerce might gain a footing
on these shores, are not remembered as they should
be by the British Government.   But it is true
that they are protected; it is feared very much
protected.   To be accurate, they are remembered
sometimes in the partitioning of their territories,
the minimising of their authority, and, worse than
all, in some cases, in the sowing of those seeds of
discord, calculated to destroy the integrity of a
people.

The work of destruction, speaking generally,
goes on not in the light of day, but, metaphorically,

in the dark hours of night.   The mighty Titan does not knock down his victim and deprive him of life outright.   Oh no! that would be too crude a way.   With the gin bottle in the one hand, and the Bible in the other, he urges moral excellence, which, in his heart of hearts, he knows to be impossible of attainment by the African under the circumstances; and when the latter fails, his benevolent protector makes such failure a cause for dismembering his tribe, alienating his lands, appropriating his goods, and sapping the foundations of his authority and institutions.   To apply Tennyson's simile, the Titan only knows what the Titan wants, or what he means.   And all the while the eternal verity remains that the natural line of development for the aborigines is racial and national, and that this is the only way to successful European intercourse and enterprise. The situation could not be better hit off than in the suggestive lines of Mr. Guy Eden who, with marvellous insight, has written in the " King of the Blacks " :

" Clad in the civilised rags of humanity,
  Blear-eyed and shaggy, he limps down the street,
Grinning about him with childish urbanity,
  Begging of all whom he chances to meet.
Begging, but not for sound garments to cover him,
  Nor for the food that he longs for, you'd think.
No, for a civilised passion is over him,
  All that he asks and he craves for is drink!

" But in the days long before the white man appeared,
  Here on this spot where a town was unknown,
Hunger and thirst were two things Billy never feared,
  Round him was plenty, and all was his own.
All was his own, for a tribe paid their court to him,
  Called him their King, in those days that are past,
Subjects in scores all their loyalty brought to him,
  First amongst men was he then—now, the last!

" Where are all they who would make such a ' bobbery,'
  Roaming the bush like glad children at play,
Where the mad whirl of the tribal ' corrobboree,'
  Where the wild chaunt at the close of the day?
Scattered and gone, for the world had no room for
    them,
    Far o'er the seas came the pitiless cry :
' Why should they live? Fate has writ large its doom
    for them,
    Land for the whites ! Let the black fellows die ! '

" ' Land for the whites ! ' Aye, the answer came speedily,
  Civilisation, with hot eager stride,
Sweeping upon them with maw gaping greedily,
  Swallowed them up in their pitiful pride.
See there the last of them, King in the days of old !
  Now 'midst the lowest he takes the last place.
Surely some day, when the story of life is told,
  Angels will weep for the last of his race ! "

But we were taking a passing view of Sekondi,
and our companion was none other than Kwamankra. We have retraced our steps over the
railway bridge, and are now in Dutch Sekondi.

On the left wing of the street are a number of
substantial business houses looking defiantly down
upon a small building of four bare walls which
represents the Wesleyan tabernacle at Sekondi.

The spot upon which this simple building
stands is historic. Here, half a century ago, was
waged the civil war between the English and the
Dutch, in which the good African missionary.
Kwamina Affua, who had been baptised by the
good missionaries as James Hayford, sometime
British Resident at Kumasi, an ancestor of
Kwamankra, and a brother of Kweku Atta, the
then Omanhin of Cape Coast, lost his life.   As
peacemaker, he had gone to help separate the com-
batants.   In the struggle he was brutally, though
perhaps, unintentionally, struck down. Peace be
to his ashes ! It is a sacred spot, and no wonder
that the stars in their courses would seem to fight
against the powers of mammon in their efforts to
dislodge the worshippers.

It being the hour of prayer, Kwamankra
followed the crowd into the holy edifice, resolved
to see for himself the result of fifty years of
missionary effort. He noticed familiar faces here
and there.   There was Kwesi Yaw, who was quite
a kid, and a carpenter's apprentice, in his school
days at Cape Coast.   How he had aged !   The
lines of care were thickly marked on his face.
Yonder was Esi Maynu, who used to be the laundry

maid at the old boarding establishment. Marks
of age were upon her too; and when he remembered
how gay and sprightly they, the young people,
were in those bygone days, a sense of sadness came
over him.

What were they doing here? They had come to
worship, of course. Did they worship, or did they
not, in those far away days when they, the young
people, joined hands together in the moonlight
under the open sky and sang *Sanko* songs? Even
then, to Kwamankra, the words of their familiar
Sanko were full of meaning; and as he listened
to-day to the wheezing sound of an old harmonium
upon which a missionary boy was performing, he
could not help thinking how much his people lost
in passing from their ways to those of the white
man. For a harmonium they had castanets with
which they kept time as one of their number, Kobina
Edu it was, gave the solo of the favourite *Sanko*
while they joined in the chorus. He remembered
the words so well, and readily recalled them :

> *Mi sankofu, wo nwhe bra yaku apa,*
> *Inwhe bra wumba arku awiay;*
> *Aryarsa, ye yi wu be ye biada!*
> *Obiri, Osawu si ay!*
> *Adapawi, osawusi,*
> *Mimpona, bada miyamu.*
> *Afi yi na nisini ya funa!*
> *Anapawi, mi dofu, mimpona ba da miyam!*

Meaning :

Companions mine, see how well we've struggled,
Behold how far thy children have striven;
If so be, we shall still struggle on!
She is black and comely, she is like unto her sire!
Morning star, thou art like unto thy sire!
My sweetheart, come to my embrace;
My Saviour, come to my bosom.
How wearied are we this season!
Morning star, sweetheart mine, beloved, come to my
    embrace!

How simple, how natural, how spontaneous all
this was compared with the refrain of " Dare to
be a Daniel," composed and sang by Ira D. Sankey,
which the missionary boy, with so much effort, was
trying to play in tune. Those were the days of
healthy Fanti manhood. The nation has missed
the promise of her prime, and is likely to bow her
gray hairs in sorrow and shame to the grave.

The congregation was composed for the most
part of children, clad each in a few fathoms of
Manchester home-spuns. At the head of the choir
was the schoolmaster whose attire certainly
invited attention. In his elegantly cut-away
black morning coat and beautifully-glazed cuffs
and collar, not to speak of patent leather shoes,
which he kept spotlessly bright by occasionally
dusting them with his pocket handkerchief, tucked
away in his shirt sleeves, he certainly looked a

F

veritable " swell," but he also did look a veritable fool.

And this was the sum total of half a century of missionary zeal and effort. Could it be for this that the simple good-hearted fathers of our race had suffered and died? They prayed for light for themselves and for their children's children. But instead of light, say ye Gods, does not darkness brood over the land?

The preacher was a white man, preaching to a black congregation; and outside on the front wall of the holy edifice was to be seen a notice which informed all whom it might concern that there would be a service *for* Europeans in the Club House at the station at a certain hour that day. Kwamankra turned away in disgust.

Later in the day he came across Essi Maynu, the selfsame laundry maid of old days. He said to her: " Do you remember me, Essi?" She looked him up and down, and made a move as if to embrace him, but she checked herself.

" What's the matter," said Kwamankra. " Does your new religion teach you to be shy of old friends? Now, to show you that I, at least, am not changed, I shall come round this evening with some of my *Sankofu*; and shan't we have a nice time with music and with dance?" She raised her eyes in holy horror as much as to say : " Get thee behind me Satan."

Kwamankra retreated like a beaten man; but the lesson was not lost on him. Henceforth he was resolved to devote the rest of his life in bringing back his people to their primitive simplicity and faith. And, in that resolve, he mused upon the words : " Bushido (Shintoism) offers us the ideal of poverty instead of wealth, humility in place of ostentation, reserve instead of reclame, self-sacrifice in place of selfishness, the care of the interest of the State rather than that of the individual. It inspires ardent courage and the refusal to turn back upon the enemy. It looks death calmly in the face, and prefers it to ignominy of any kind. It preaches submission to authority and the sacrifice of all private interests, whether of self or of family, to the common weal. It requires its disciples to submit to a strict physical and mental discipline, develops a martial spirit, and by lauding the virtues of courage, constancy, fortitude, faithfulness, daring, self-restraint, offers an exalted code of moral principles, not only for the man and the warrior, but for men and women in times both of peace and war."

" That is it; that is it; I have it," said Kwamankra. " If my people are to be saved from national and racial death, they must be proved as if by fire—by the practice of a virile religion, not by following emasculated sentimentalities which men shamelessly and slanderously identify with the holy One of God, His son, Jesus Christ."

CHAPTER VI.

THE WORLD, THE FLESH AND THE DEVIL.

CHAPTER VI.

THE WORLD, THE FLESH AND THE DEVIL.

1.

FOR the Rev. Silas Whitely the die was cast. Passing from college to ordination without any fixed ideas as to his own relation to God in his son Jesus Christ, or otherwise, and yielding to the advice of an old college chum, Kennedy Bilcox by name, who at this time was holding the post of Political Officer on the Gold Coast, he had made up his mind to put in an application for the Colonial Chaplaincy at Sekondi rather than continue to face a life of penury as a curate in East London, particularly as he knew a friend or two who would work the back door influence beautifully with the officials at the Colonial Office on his behalf.

"And what is the screw like," eagerly asked Whitely, when Bilcox first made the suggestion to him.

"Oh, it is only a matter of some five hundred a year with an annual rise of twenty-five pounds, until you reach six hundred pounds, besides fees and allowances thrown in here and there, passages

in and out free every twelve months, etcetera,
etcetera, etcetera, with an assistant chaplain, a
black man of course, to save you unnecessary
drudgery.''

'' That is quite good enough for me, minus the
etceteras, and I am sure I thank you from the
bottom of my heart for giving me an inkling of
such a billet. By George! how spoilt you Colonials
are; and to think I was going to immure myself
in East London for the rest of my natural life'! ''

'' But, remember,'' put in Bilcox, '' you will be
subject to discipline. You must not, for example,
join the silly band of 'progressives,' or your
chances of promotion will be absolutely nil, and
you may even run the risk of being shelved altogether. The process of shelving is a simple one.
You get down with fever; you are invalided home;
you never return again, that is all.''

'' You needn't fear about that. I have no pro-
clivities that way, but tell me all about the
'progressives' on the Gold Coast.''

'' Why, they are a mere handful of white fools
who are blind enough not to see where their bread
is buttered, and who advocate equal rights for the
native, and all that sort of tommy rot. Now,
between ourselves,'' breaking out into a low mischievous laugh, '' the Lieutenant-Governor himself had progressive leanings when he first came
out among us, and would not take the advice of us,

old coasters.   He seemed then as if he could **dine**
off niggers, pardon a bit of Coast slang, until **he**
was bitten, and bitten pretty sharply too, **I can**
tell you.   Now he sings the ' progressive ' **tune**
no longer," laying particular emphasis on the **last**
sentiment.

" But how was he bitten, and by whom? "

" By tho Fantis, of course.   Didn't you **read**
in the papers at the time how he was hooted **by**
the Fanti women in the central province?   I was
for bombarding their stronghold and sending the
niggers flying all over the country, but the old
bounder, the Permanent Secretary at the Colonial
Office, who, by the way, is the one who really rules
the roost, wouldn't let us.   The thing is too bad,
to think of niggers hooting a Lieutenant-
Governor."

" I confess, Bilcox, I cannot see the magnitude
of the offence.   I suppose there must have been
something to hoot the good Governor for."

" Oh, it was all about the Provincial Council
question," answered Bilcox, wearily, as if struck
by a sudden thought.   " I must be going home now.
My little daughter will be all eagerness to welcome
her papa.   I came up to London to draw my pay,
and meeting old coasters seems always to arouse
the brute part of one somehow."

" How do you mean, Bilcox? " said Whitely.
" Surely you must have a better account of your
fellows than that."

Bilcox, ignoring the thrust, said in a sad tone :
" You know, Whitely, sometimes I cannot stand
the funny little questions my little daughter puts
to me when I return home from Africa. She has
an idea that God has made of one blood all nations
to dwell on the face of the earth—you know the
quotation; it is more in your line. I don't know
whence she got the notion, but, ' papa,' she would
jump on my knee, and looking me straight in the
face with her delicate blue eyes, ' papa,' she would
begin, ' I hope you were very good to those poor
African people whom you have to look after.
They say they are sometimes badly treated, but
you will be kind to them, won't you ? ' When I
am alone, I do think of these things, and my better
self whispers to me that the child's sentiments are
right, and that they are directly contradictory to
my line of official work."

" There is a good deal in what you say. To be
frank, Bilcox, I must say I cannot see, for instance, why sensible men should go into hysterics
because a Lieutenant-Governor was hooted at.
Why, I was at a meeting the other day at the
Queen's Hall when Mr. Balfour was hissed at, and
for a considerable length of time he could not get
a hearing. I don't remember the Hussars being
called out to punish the naughty little band of
British barbarians, as Grant Allen good-humouredly dubs us. And mind you he was the Prime
Minister."

"Perhaps that is the reasonable way of looking at the matter, but we all suffer from an affliction known as Coast conscience, and the powers save you, if you, as parson, should get a touch of it when you get out there. As for myself, I shall go quite crazy one of these days, if I don't soon give up this job."

In due course the Rev. Silas Whitely received his appointment as Colonial Chaplain of Sekondi, nor did he find the emoluments of the office in any way exaggerated by his friend the Political Officer. His mother was satisfied, but to do the reverend gentleman justice, before sailing out, his own heart was full of misgiving first as to his own spiritual condition, secondly as to whether he would have the moral courage, in the face of official stress, to do his duty as a man. A few months of coast life, however, soon settled all his doubts. Why should he worry about the matter of his spiritual condition. He was not the first clergyman who had been troubled with conscientious scruples. He would go through the ordinary routine of his work, and, when his term was ended, he would pack up his traps and go. Besides, it appeared that he had set too high an estimate upon the black character. The blacks, he had come to consider, were nothing but a pack of dishonest people, robbing white traders right and left, smuggling contraband goods, and defrauding His

Majesty's Government whenever they could. His
duty as a Colonial Chaplain was plain. He must
teach these people the elementary principles of
honesty, thereby working hand in hand with His
Majesty's judges who had arrived at the same
result. It was true there were a few exceptions
among the educated class, but he was beginning
to entertain doubts as to how to place even that
class, and he was not at all sure how he would
receive Kwamankra even, whom he assured himself he had known just slightly in the 'Varsity, if
he happened to meet him on the Gold Coast.

The Assistant Colonial Chaplain was the Rev.
Kwaw Baidu, who drew an annual stipend of one
hundred and fifty pounds. Besides doing the
pastoral work along the railway line, including
the management of a mission at Tarkwa, he had
the bulk of the chaplaincy work thrown upon him,
while the Chaplain himself was content to draw
his fat pay and take things easy, as, he took care
to explain, the medical officer had advised him to
do as little as possible on account of the dreadful
climate. Outside purely official duties, the Colonial Chaplain had nothing to do with his assistant,
who was a highly cultured man, and, in some respects, his senior, having taken a better degree
than the Chaplain. Not that the Chaplain was in
any way unkind to the Assistant Chaplain. Oh,
dear no! He only wished it to be mutually under-

stood that between them was a natural gulf fixed
—the gulf of a difference in their respective social
status. So that if the twain happened to be at
work together at the chaplaincy, and the Super-
visor of Customs, let us say, called, he would
politely say: "Mr. Baidu, would you kindly
excuse me, you will find the verandah cool and
comfortable," and would never venture upon an
introduction.

The Rev. Kwaw Baidu was an humble-minded
man, and so long as the Colonial Chaplain did not
come in conflict with him upon matters of principle, he did not mind. But, at last, an occasion
for stumbling and a rock of offence arose in the
shape of the segregation question. The town of
Akrokeri had been laid out into a European
quarter immediately fronting the railway, and
occupying the finest site the neighbourhood
yielded, while the native chief and his people who
by rights should own the whole surface, save such
as was actually required for building purposes by
the mines, had, with the connivance of the Government, been located on the steeps of a line of hills
to the east, for which they had to pay quarterly
rent. But when the question of building a cemetery for the interment of Akrokerites arose, and
the European inhabitants put forward the view
that on no account would they commingle their
dead with the dead of " niggers," and the matter

was by the Political Officer referred to the chaplaincy for opinion, the Rev. Silas Whitely held that the Europeans were right, and the thing put the Rev. Kwaw Baidu's back up.

"Do you mean to say, you an ambassador of Jesus Christ, that you are going to support any such nonsense as this which knocks the bottom out of all Christian charity? No wonder that the people turn a deaf ear to all my appeals. I will speak plainly to you for once. If you do not yield to reason and the spirit of Christ, whom you and I profess to follow, I will report your conduct to the Bishop, and, if need be, I will appeal to the Archbishop of Canterbury."

"You may do what you like, Mr. Baidu, but you seem to forget that this is a British Colony, and that the salaries of you and me are paid by the Colonial Government, and not by the Archbishop of Canterbury. Besides, I consider your opposition a piece of impertinence, and you must consider yourself suspended until I have recommended your dismissal to headquarters."

In due course the Rev. Kwaw Baidu was compulsorily retired from the Colonial service, and a path, thirty-six feet wide, was marked between the European and native cemeteries, and the former beautifully fenced in with money mostly contributed by the black folk. But the matter got noised abroad, and there wasn't a soul in the diocese of Sekondi that did not come to know of it.

2.

A decrepit old woman, limping heavily on her crutches, made her way into the chaplaincy yard and insisted upon speaking to the white chaplain.

The chaplaincy yard was kept scrupulously clean, and the little garden adjacent, with hybiscus and crotons growing in rich profusion, and all bordered with festoons of sweet-peas and scarlet runners in early bloom, showed, as clearly as outside appearances went, that the Rev. Silas Whitely fully appreciated the good things of life.

The Colonial Chaplain had dined well, and was enjoying a Havana under the spreading bread-fruit trees which adorned the chaplaincy yard. The full moon threw a spray of silvery light through the myriad leaves of the overspreading branches, casting a halo over his face quite out of keeping with the mundane thoughts which at the moment engaged the mind of the reverend gentleman.

" Yes, I believe in even an ambassador of Christ having a good time. Why should I be such a silly ass as to refuse a whisky and soda at the Club? Besides, we must be all things unto all men. That is clearly the scriptural admonition, and it suits my present humour down to the ground. So there goes it; it is done "—this as he flicked off the live ashes from his cigar.

A deep, low cough arrested the attention of the Rev. Silas Whitely, and he turned to see the direction whence it came. He had thought he was alone.

" Was it you, Nancy? " he said, addressing the old woman. " What brings you here to-night? "

The woman addressed curtsied low. She had been brought up in the Mission school, finishing up in the High School, and spoke English with remarkable fluency. She had loved, and she had lost—first husband, then an only son who had been unto the husband as the apple of the eye, and, therefore, doubly dear unto her woman's heart. Did I say lost? No, they were not lost. At least thus she had been taught by the missionaries, and when she was sad the chaplain had cheered her with the hope of the resurrection morn. She had come to believe that somewhere, in another sphere, they awaited her; and her one thought was that happy hour, one day, when they would welcome her to a place beside them. She lived for this, and worked for this hope. Now and again she thought she had glimpses of Him who said : " I am the Way, the Truth, and the Life," and she had been told the way to Him was to maintain the truth. A heavy burden, for some time back, had sorely pressed upon her heart, which she felt would be lifted by telling the Rev. Silas Whitely the truth, as she conceived it; and so here she was to do it, and yet did not know how.

A soft wind rustled the luxuriant foliage over-
head, and through the branches the bright stars
peeped down upon this simple old woman whose
only wish was to be in harmony with Nature's
God. A sudden inspiration, like the wind blowing where it listeth, came to her. She would tell
the chaplain a story, as she had heard he was fond
of Fanti stories, and was wont to collect them; and
what better time than a moonlight night in Africa
for telling stories?

Nancy laid aside her crutches, took a low stool
offered her by the Chaplain, and cleared her throat
of a troublesome cough or two. " I have a nice
story to tell you, sir, to add to your collection, and,
as I was feeling a little stronger this evening than
usual, I thought I would come in."

" Certainly, quite welcome," said the Rev. Silas
Whitely. " Fire away, Nancy; I am all eagerness to hear you begin."

" Once upon a time," Nancy began in a clear,
sonorous voice, "there went into a far distant
country two Mahomedan priests to work for Allah.
After a time their paths lay in different districts,
and they seldom heard of one another. As was
their wont, the missionaries worked in leather and
other useful industries; but, as it happened, Akarbah succeeded and grew rich in worldly goods,
while Adaku, his friend, merely lived from hand
to mouth; yet did Allah bless his labours. As is

the way of the world, Akarbah's society was now sought by the highest in the land; and when he counted his beads at the hour of prayer, he failed not to thank Allah for all the good He gave.

" One day as he returned from the house of prayer he met an errand boy, who handed him a bit of parchment, written in Arabic. He opened it, and found it was a message from his brother missionary, who, he knew, was low and humble in the things of this world. ' This day,' so the message ran, ' I, Adaku, thy brother missionary, shall lodge with thee.'

" Akarbah frowned. It was very inconvenient. This very day the High Sheriff was to dine with him, the rich and prosperous Akarbah, and what would he say if he met at his table a mendicant friar of a Mahomedan priest? He was resolved. The thing must not be. ' Here, lad, take this parchment back quickly to my brother Adaku. Make sure and give it to him, and I will give you my blessing and a silver piece upon your return.'

" The lad ran past the camels and the horses and the cattle in the market places, and went out by the fifth gate of the city to find the priest Adaku was not at the place where he expected him to be. Adaku had already entered by the seventh gate, and was already within the holy precincts of the abode of Akarbah.

" ' Hail, brother,' was Adaku's salutation. ' May Allah be ever more gracious to thee.'

"For answer Akarbah visibly trembled with agitation. ' Did you not receive the parchment ? ' Adaku stared vacantly at his friend. ' What parchment ? '

" Akarbah gave no answer, but suddenly left the precincts of his abode, as if struck by a sudden thought. The hours passed, but they did not bring Akarbah. At last the truth dawned upon Adaku. ' Evidently I am not wanted here,' and, putting on his sandals and snatching his staff, he passed out of the house of his friend, shaking the dust off his feet as he did so, and never forgetting to mention him, not in anger, it is said, when he counted his beads in the house of Allah."

" What a funny story, Nancy; whatever do you mean ? " said the Rev. Silas Whitely, as the old woman finished what she had to say.

" Yes, it is funny," she said; " but you know, chaplain, I have lately had such grave doubts as to whether what you tell us in those beautiful sermons you read out every Sunday about the love of God, of heaven, and the rest of it can all be true; and oh ! whatever shall I do after all these years of weary waiting, if they are not true ? Where is my husband, and where my son ? " and it was painful to see the distress and the anguish in the face of the poor woman.

" Don't go on like that, Nancy. But what is there to make you doubt of heaven and the love of God ? "

G

The old woman dried a tear or two, and said very slowly and deliberately :

"Chaplain, you asked me when I had done telling my story what I meant by it. I have prayed to God night and day for some time to be able to answer that self-same question when it came, and now, God helping me, I will. Know thou, then, that thou art the Akarbah of my story. God hath exalted you above thy fellows that thou mightest be a guide unto us his forlorn little ones, and show us the way of love and the way to heaven. But surely thou hast not dealt in love with thy brother, Kwaw Baidu, who is now out of work, with wife and children depending upon him, whose story is known to all the parishioners for miles and miles around. And oh! if the heaven you have so often preached about hath two ways leading to it, one for us black folk and one for you our masters, what an undesirable place it must be for us after all the weariness here below. But do tell me—you who have raised the hope in me—where is now my husband, and where my child?" ejaculated the poor woman, wringing her hands. "Tell me, for thou hast helped to raise false hopes in me. Oh, God! what shall I do?" And the poor woman swooned away in a dead faint. Every effort was made to revive her, without success, and when the doctor arrived he pronounced life extinct.

CHAPTER VII.

Signs of Empire : Loyal Hearts.

It was Empire Day—the 24th of May—the day on which was commemorated throughout the Empire the birth of the great white Queen who, in her life, surrounded the British throne with a halo of womanly virtues, the kind of thing before which, in all ages and in all climes, the heart of universal man bows low in reverential homage and respect.

The Gold Coast is also a component part of the British Empire—as necessary to the complete whole as the smallest link to the complete chain; and so, as the women trooped out this morning in their hundreds in Ethiopian costumes with their hair done up in the most graceful, yet picturesque, fashions, and the children with bunting and palms and flowers, all gay and merry as for a wedding feast, one could easily realise that the heart of the people was true. What could not be made of material such as this—the nucleus of the free Ethiopian Empire that is to be?

Why had they thus turned out? What meaning had "Empire Day" for these simple folk?

G 2

All they knew was that the great white Queen, the great *Awuraba*, or mistress, whose son now reigned over them, had been born on this day, and her they delighted to honour; but if you asked them wherefore they loved and cherished her memory, they could not tell you why. Perhaps it was an instinctive feeling that she, a good woman, could never be unkind to them and their people, and sympathy had begotten loyalty. After she was gone, they familiarly referred to her, and said : " *Inde Awuraba niba adzi adzi, wo ma ye nkoko sumunu,*" that was to say, " Now our mistress's son reigns; let us go and serve him."

It was a day to be remembered by the merchant, because he lost money by the closure of his factory; by the official, because it gave him a day off and extra drinks; by the school children, because they came in for a treat gratuitously supplied by the simple folk of the community, as a kind of offering to the great white throne. And so it happened that all had enjoyed themselves and made merry.

By Kenny Bilcox this day of days had been spent in looking over the District Record Book for the past six months during which he had been away on furlough. He was to take charge on the morrow, as his assistant was due for leave. But the more he read the more furious did he become. Things had not altogether gone to his liking. It

was late in the afternoon; the day had been sultry;
and he, faithful servant of the King, had worked
late and long. Suddenly, turning round to his
orderly : " Kwesi," he said, " run fast, fast, to
Mr. Macan and tell him I want him here one
time."

" Yes, Sar!" and, in a moment, Kwesi was
racing down the main street in the direction of the
parade ground.

"Maser want you, sar," said Kwesi to Macan,
who was enjoying himself immensely in his own
fashion.

" And what on earth does ' maser ' want with
me on a day like this? Say to ' maser ' I dey
come."

" Tut! tut! tut! whatever good are you for, I
should like to know," said Political Officer Bilcox
to his assistant, David Macan, as in return to a
low respectful bow, he merely glanced Macan's
way in a half nod, half menace. " The fact is,"
he pursued, " you are too d—m straight for the
Gold Coast Diplomatic Service. It is like you
Scotch people, you are always putting your confounded conscience before obvious duty. Here
you have gone and spoilt a whole eighteen months
of strenuous work on my part to put into operation in Insima District the policy mapped out by
the Lieutenant-Governor."

David Macan was somewhat taken aback at

this sort of reception, and, at first, did not know whether to put it down to the extra rise in the thermometer, extra whiskies and sodas, or to his ill luck in being born with a conscience. Truth to tell, David Macan was a typical Scotchman, as straight as a die, and had already gained for himself among the Africans the sobriquet of " honest David." Reflecting a moment, David said, " Excuse me, sir, but I don't know in the least what you are talking about. Perhaps if you took the matter calmly, I can understand you better. In the meanwhile, let me warn you, sir," his Scotch blood for the nonce getting the better of him, " that much as I respect you, I shall seriously resent the next rash reference you make to my people."

" And what on earth do you mean by allowing that impudent rascal Kwamankra to sneak into this district?" angrily demanded Bilcox, and ignoring Macan's remonstrance. " We'll have our hands full, I can assure you, and you will have to answer for it at headquarters. But whether or not, I won't have you in this district, do you hear? I'll recommend you for leave at once, and when you return, if you ever do, you may go to Kintampor, or some hotter place, for aught I care."

" How absurd you are this evening, Mr. Bilcox, to be sure! How could I prevent Kwamankra coming into the district to practise? Besides, he is a native of the country; the chiefs look up to him; and I had always understood we were to work through the chiefs, and, by parity of reasoning, through their natural leaders.''

'' Do you call it sound policy to play into the hands of a man who can write such rubbish as this Kwamankra does?'' throwing heavily upon the table a thick volume which had been standing on the dirty shelf. '' Pray listen to this and tell me whether your senses have fled,'' this as he read from the open page the following : '' ' Were there such a thing as political ethics, or a pretence or semblance thereof among Christian nations, as there is a semblance of some sort of Christianity in so-called Christian countries, it might be permissible to inquire how far the conduct of Christian nations in relation to aboriginal races, sometimes charitably called subject races, conformed to the Christian standard of morality—' Now that is rank heresy, teaching the aboriginals that we are a parcel of hypocrites and cut-throats; and to think that the writer of this vile stuff has been let in here through your stupidity!'' pursued Bilcox breathlessly.

Macan made a move as if to knock the Political Officer down; but just then a voice from the verandah attracted his attention, and, in a twinkling, Whitely had placed himself between the two.

"There is no reason," said Whitely, "why you two gentlemen should not repair to the back yard and have it out in true sportsmanlike fashion. But as for expressing your opinions of one another freely in the hearing of the black boys, I don't know what to say of it. By George! how they swarmed at the foot of the stairs, peeping one behind the other, until I kicked them off the premises as I came up. Besides, we did the thing differently in my youthful days. Fewer words, you know; but, perhaps, the heat had something to do with it, or I mightn't have had the trouble of interfering," placing himself in pugilistic attitude first towards Bilcox, and then towards Macan. The situation was fast bordering on the ridiculous, and as Macan was in no mood for fun, he snatched up his hat, bowed low, and in a moment he was gone.

"B—oy! b—oy! cocktails, two cocktails, do you hear? and look sharp about it, or by Jove, I will break every bone in your body!" Then turning to Whitely—"The idea of these boys always hanging round and eavesdropping. The worst of it is one can't do without them."

When the servant had placed the drinks on the table and departed, Whitely said: "I would advise you, Bilcox, to be careful what you say in the hearing of these native boys of the man Kwamankra. You have no idea what a hold he has upon the popular imagination, and how wide-spread is his influence.   Personally, there is some-thing irresistible about him I could never with-stand. I knew him in my student days.   Under normal conditions, I should say it is the charm of a manly purpose and force of character.   But, then, no one is normal in these parts."   And there was a strange sadness in his voice which Bilcox could not help noticing from the way he laid stress on the words " no one."

" Mind you don't miss the Chief Magistrate's dinner, or he'll never forgive you; the hour is 8 p.m.," said Whitely, as he slowly descended the stairs.

As for Macan, he could not help turning over in his mind the strange medley which was labelled the Gold Coast Diplomatic Service.   He remem-bered reading somewhere before coming out the following : " *It must strike the careful observer that the position of a man in the public service of the Gold Coast is often a difficult one.   If such a man is honest and intelligent, he cannot fail soon to discover the peculiar conditions under which he is called upon to discharge his duties.   The first thing that will occur to him will be the dog-in-the-manger policy of the Administration, whose servant he is.   He will find that, theoretically, the people are free, having their own laws and institutions.   He will see that the*

Government, apparently, recognise this fact; but that in practice, he, the public servant, is expected to interfere with the institutions of the people as far as he dares. Neither is he told to allow the natural development of the institutions of the people, nor is he directed, in so many words, to attempt to mould them. What he does to-day, which is considered wrong by his superiors, may be done to-morrow by another and applauded." As he put two and two together, trying to fathom the real cause of his superior officer's annoyance, the truth gradually dawned upon him. He had acted by the natives as an honest man should do. During the time he had acted as the head of the Diplomatic Service he had given the chiefs every encouragement to unite with one another and to consolidate their authority and jurisdiction over their people. He had encouraged national schools throughout the district, and supported the Chiefs to make bye-laws, requiring every child to attend the schools until the age of fourteen. All these were in the line of normal and healthy growth of the people in enlightened progressive ways, and he had worked with a will and a great deal of intelligence and tact. It had never dawned upon him that there was a theoretical policy and a practical one, the latter having as its aim such a shaping of circumstances as would for ever make

the Ethiopian in his own country a hewer of wood
and a drawer of water unto his Caucasian protector and so-called friend.   This then was what he
was expected to do.   Was it right, could he con-
scientiously do it?

CHAPTER VIII.

A MAGISTERIAL FUNCTION.

CHAPTER VIII.

A MAGISTERIAL FUNCTION.

A SPLENDID repast, in the course of which good spirits and good cheer had flowed freely. The talk had varied from Oxford dons to Japanese admirals and Russian generals; and when it came down to liqueur and coffee everyone was merry, but truly the merriest was the genial host, and a right down good sort he was.

The Chief Magistrate beat himself this evening, and as he waxed more and more eloquent and glibly passed on from one subject to the other, it was only right that the eternal race question should come in for a fair consideration.

They were a body of learned men, the guests of the evening, including the members of the Diplomatic Service, one or two doctors, with a fair sprinkling of coloured barristers, and, as it became such a company, they talked learnedly.

" When you come to talk of the jurisdiction of the native Kings and Chiefs I lose all patience with you," said the host, as he wheeled round upon a youthful barrister who had ventured to make an observation upon the destoolment, that is to say, the deposition of the Chief of Agona. " The

King of England is King here, and it is ridiculous
to think that these little squirts of puppet head-
men can be said to have jurisdiction."

Macan of the Diplomatic Service rashly came
to the rescue of the youthful barrister. " I
thought I had seen such a thing as a Native Jurisdiction Ordinance in the *Corpus Juris* of the Gold
Coast."

The host growled and told him plainly, but
politely, without much ado, that he knew next
to nothing about the matter. Turning to Kwamankra, he pursued, " Now, what do you think—
you go up country, and one day one of your puppet
kings sends and arrests you and claps you in gaol
--how would you feel over the matter, eh ? "

" At the best of times, I confess," said Kwamankra, " it is not pleasant to find oneself in
durance vile. But if the jurisdiction is there,
what is there to do but to submit to it ? "

" That is exactly what you needn't do. When
one of your native authorities comes before me
with their confounded jurisdiction notions I treat
them as little children, and dismiss the whole
thing with a jest. I can assure you, it is a most
effective way. Besides, talking seriously, you have
not considered the effect of the Order in Council."

" Which Order in Council do you mean ? " ventured a precocious full-fledged.

" What else can I mean but the last, which de-

fined the limits of the colony, and vested the jurisdiction in our sovereign Lord the King," almost
shrieked out the host.

" My dear sir," put in Kwamankra, " if I may
venture to come to the assistance of my young
friend, it takes two to make a bargain, as you will
find if you examine into the constitutional history
of the country."

For the moment the host was nonplussed. He
was somewhat hazy as to the historical part of
the subject. But as a parting shell, he exclaimed :
" Well, be that as it may, it was one of your own
men who drew a report upon this very matter upon
which the Government have acted. I have seen it
with my own eyes, I assure you, and I make you
a present of the fact."

" I say, Whitely," continued the Chief Magistrate, " how did you get on with that cemetery
controversy of yours ? I hear you have given your
assistant the sack. I say, it is really too bad of
you. I am strong on so-called native jurisdiction,
and that kind of thing, but when it comes to segregation of the dead, I tell you the thing beats me.
Think of old Lawson, the pioneer of the gold in-
dustry, not receiving decent interment on the
ground of colour. The thing is preposterous, and
I am not in sympathy with it." Whitely coloured
up and appeared confused. The criticism was
sharp and unexpected.

The Chief Magistrate was known for his frank
expression of opinion, no matter what the subject
matter of discussion was. Bilcox thought it was
time he came to the rescue of the Government
policy.

"Bravo! Chief, I like your fine speech,"
addressing the Chief Magistrate. "I never knew
you were a champion of the non-segregation
theory. At the next sitting of the Council I shall
not fail to record the considered views of such a
highly placed official as your Honour."

"I have never been able to understand the
argument in favour of segregation," put in the
conscientious Macan unguardedly. "In the
time of an epidemic, for instance, I can understand why the afflicted, without distinction,
should be put away. But in normal times, to be
sure, I don't understand the philosophy of the
matter."

"The question has nothing to do with epi-
demics. The man in the street knows that,"
sourly retorted Bilcox. "Besides, it is common
knowledge that whites never catch small-pox from
blacks," he added irrelevantly.

"Ha! ha! ha! ha!" burst out Dr. Castor.
"That's good, go one further. In all my experience I declare!"

"You don't mean to insult me, doctor, I hope.
Besides, all this discussion before these gentle-

men," waving his hand in the direction of the coloured fraternity, " is most unseemly, and I for one must beg leave to retire."

" Pray, don't go away, Mr. Bilcox," said Kwamankra.   " I am sure we are not offended in the slightest.   My friends here, like myself, are used to this kind of thing.   But what are the odds?   I, for one, am strong on *reciprocity*."

" And what has reciprocity to do with this matter? " angrily demanded the Political Officer.

" Only this, sir," began Kwamankra calmly, " that if you took mankind in the aggregate, irrespective of race, and shook them up together, as you would the slips of paper in a jury panel box, you would find after the exercise that the cultured would shake themselves free and come together, and so would the uncouth, the vulgar, and the ignorant; but, of course, you would ignore this law of nature, and, with a wave of the hand, confine the races in separate air-tight compartments. Wherefore I preach *reciprocity*."

" I say, you fellows, we must be going; it is getting late "—this said the senior member of the legal fraternity as he rose, turban in hand, to take leave of the genial host, who was fuming at Bilcox's rudeness.   " Good-night, sir, we thank you so much for kind entertainment," he continued, addressing the Chief Magistrate.

" Good-night, gentlemen."

H

CHAPTER IX.

THE YELLOW PERIL.

CHAPTER IX.

The Yellow Peril.

The political wisdom of Ekra Kwow, the son of Kwamankra, was learnt at the feet of his father while yet he was in his teens. Being a lad of inquiring mind and quick perception, many a curious question did he put to his father on odd occasions, when Kwamankra would return answers full of pith and marrow.

" What is the meaning of the ' yellow peril ' ? " interrogated the precocious youth, as he craned his neck behind the chair of the paterfamilias, who was leisurely gleaning from the pages of *Public Opinion*.

Kwamankra raised his eyes from the printed matter, and beckoned the young hopeful forward. Eyeing the lad curiously, he said, " If you must know, I suppose I must give you the lesson, and, perhaps, the earlier the better. Now, if you should be going to school to-morrow, and at the street corner Kweku Mensah knocked off your cap and punched your nose, what would you do ? "

" I would, of course, punch his head back," answered the lad triumphantly.

" Good ! Now let us go a step further. Suppose

H 2

your school fellows were going on a picnic, and
Kobina Tsintsin's boys met you on the public road
and barred your progress, would not you brave
lads fight your way through?"

"Of course, dad, what else could we do in
honour of our school?"

"Now, for the application. In geography
books you have learnt that different nations dwell
on the face of the earth—white, yellow, red, brown
and black like ourselves. They each occupy a
portion of the earth's surface. Those who occupy
those tiny islands somewhere in the English
Channel are, as you know, called the English. So
you have the Japanese, those brave fellows, the
Indians, the Africans, or to come down to particulars, among the Africans, say, the Zulus, the
Ashantis, and the Fantis. To give the principle
which made you punch Kweku Mensah back, and
your school fellows bravely break through the
ranks of Kobina Tsintsin's boys, a name, let us
call it the law of self-preservation. Now, if you
relax the practice of this principle in the course
of life, you go under, and men then talk of the
survivors as the *fittest*, because they have resisted
best. You remember those lines in Shakespeare
you were reciting to me the other day :

        '   .   .   .   .   Beware
    Of entrance to a quarrel; but being in,
    Bear't that the opposed may beware of thee—'.

That is a wholesome rule of life, my boy. Well,"
pursued Kwamankra, "there are certain nations
in the world who call themselves Christians, and
who claim a monopoly of culture, knowledge and
civilisation, and who, *ergo*, think that they have a
heaven-born right to survive and thrive while all
others go under. They are mostly whites, and
when either the brown, or the yellow, or the black
man resists and shows he does not mean to go
under, these self-same white Christian people
hysterically cry out : ' The Yellow Peril,' or the
' Black Peril,' as the case may be. Do you understand, my lad ? " laying his hand slowly on the
child's head, and looking him straight in the face,
so that the child's eyes met the father's fully and
meaningly.

" Yes, I do, dad," replied the lad. " But tell
me, dad, I did not wish to interrupt you before—
why did you call the Japs, ' those brave fellows ? ' "

" Why, simply because in the present contest
they are engaged in with Russia, they have shown
they do not mean to go under, whoever else may
do so; and they have caused the cry of ' the yellow
peril ' of late to go up more hysterically than
ever. Listen to this rare bit," said Kwamankra,
reaching for his scrap album and turning to the
letter J : " The sacred duty is incumbent upon us,
as the leading state of Asiatic progress to stretch
a helping hand to China, India, and Korea, to all

the Asiatics who have confidence in us, and who are capable of civilisation. As their more powerful friend, we desire them all to be free from the yoke which Europe has placed upon them, and that they, may hereby prove to the world that the Orient is capable of measuring swords with the Occident on any field of battle." These words were spoken in the Japanese House of Peers, and they embody the principle I have been trying to inculcate upon you in a nutshell. You will do well to remember them all your life; and since I find you an apt pupil likely to pass the lessons on to others after I am gone, I will tell you of my experiences with the Political Officer."

"But what is a Political Officer?" queried the stripling.

"There you are again with your inquiring little brain. I must begin from premises to conclusion, step by step, like the *quod erat demonstrandum* you were worrying me with the other day. Still you are right, my boy. Once define clearly, and all difficulties vanish, as mist before the noon-day sun. Well, the system of Government under which we, the people of the Gold Coast, live is known as the ' Crown Colony system.' It is a system somewhat behind the times. Now, what would you boys think of your schoolmaster in these enlightened days if he should, from time to time, ask you to contribute out of your pocket money funds for the laying out of a recreation ground without allowing some of you boys to have a say as to how things were to be done, and what games were to be bought for the school? I am sure you would all revolt and say, ' If you are going to use our money, you might at least let us say what games we would like.' Under the system I am telling you of the schoolmaster is the Governor, and the lads are the people of this country whose contributions are in the shape of the heavy duties they pay on all imported articles. But they have no voice in the spending of their contributions, and that is why I say the system is somewhat behind the times. To proceed, seeing there must be discontent among the people, the Political Officer is the man appointed to deal with cases arising out of such discontent."

" But how? I don't quite understand, dad. Does he go and speak kindly to the people and tell them not to mind, and that they will have the value of their contributions, if they are patient? "

Kwamankra burst out hilariously, and for some minutes could not control himself. The lad began to feel sheepish, and thought he must have said something very odd. But, presently Kwamankra came to, and a look of sadness seemed to play upon his countenance as slowly he murmured to himself the words :

' And its heart as pure as now.'

Quick as thought, memory had flashed back that unique chapter in his life's experience when she and he had watched over this very child in infant slumbers, bone of their bone, flesh of their flesh, and in the fulness of their hearts the prayer had gone up :

> "That when time's mystic fingers wrote manhood
>   on its brow,
>   It's deeds might be as gentle and its heart as
>   pure as now."

And now, he was left alone to help realise that prayer in the youthful enquirer. Mastering his feelings, and, for the moment rolling a stone over the sepulchre of the ever virgin past, Kwamankra turned to his son, and drawing him closely to his heart, spoke gently thus : " How I wish I could keep you, my boy, from knowing the seamy side of life. But since knowledge must come some day, it were well I guided thee to the sources thereof, if so be it might not be all gall to thy thirsty soul."

" No, the Political Officer does not exactly do what one should think, my boy. Here on the Gold Coast the people have also shown that they do not mean to go under, but in a different way. You know the story of the wolf and the lamb. I see you are all eagerness. Well, it will bear repetition. The wolf meets the lamb on a thirsty day by a stream. The wolf stands higher up the stream and drinks, while the lamb quenches its thirst in the lower part. Presently Mr. Wolf says to Master Lamb, ' what do you mean by making the stream muddy ? ' ' How can that be ? ' says Master Lamb, ' since you are higher up the stream than I am.' ' I hear you spoke disrespectfully of me three months ago,' puts in Mr. Wolf. Master Lamb meekly : ' I have been in the world only two months gone.' ' Well, if it wasn't you,' replies the wolf, ' it must have been your father who did.' "

" Coward ! " cried Ekra Kwow, excitedly. " Don't I wish I were close by with my little pop gun ? I should have put a hole through Mr. Wolf right enough."

" Good, my boy, that's well said. But, unfortunately, it is an every day occurrence in this world, and, what is worse, we can't always bring to play our pop guns when we may morally be justified in doing so."

" But it is high time you were in bed. Another time, if you are good, I will tell you all about the Political Officer, and my experiences with him, if you remind me how far we have come to-day."

" Good-night, dad ! "

" Good-night, my boy," and, in a minute, he had disappeared behind the curtains, leaving Kwamankra to his thoughts and to his pipe.

CHAPTER X.

THE BLACK PERIL.

CHAPTER X.

THE BLACK PERIL.

" HERE, on the Gold Coast, the people have shown that they do not mean to go under, but in a different way— " this, as the precocious youth produced a sheet of paper with the words neatly written down. " I meant not to forfeit the rest of the story you see, dad, and now for your promise please," drawing a low seat close to the paternal chair.

" I see you have forgotten the illustration but not the text, and as other illustrations are easy to find," said Kwamankra, " I shall redeem my promise. They are scattered over the pages of history. In your historical lessons you have undoubtedly heard of what is called the 'Eastern Question?' "

" Yes, I have, though I forget what it was exactly, and, besides, I learn these things better when you tell them to me your way, dad," said the lad excitedly.

" Now, if you will compose yourself, and

remember that the story is in illustration of the discussion with which we started, namely, the so-called ' yellow peril,' you will listen to good purpose, my boy.''

The youth bowed assent, and Kwamankra began : '' It was all the doing of the Russians at the start.   Years ago they were confined in one corner of Asia Minor, having no access to the North Sea, the Baltic, or the Black Sea.   By-and-by the Emperor, Peter the Great, conceived the idea of Russian expansion toward the Crimea and northward to the Baltic.   After him Catherine II. of Russia sought to carry into effect the dream of Peter the Great, and thenceforth it became the national policy of the Russian Bear.''

'' What do you mean by the Russian Bear ? ''

'' It means the Russian in the sense in which we talk of John Bull.''

'' Oh ! go on dad.''

'' Well, in the pursuit of this policy by the Russian Bear, she came in collision with the Turk in the Crimea about the time of the Emperor Nicolas II. in the fifties of the last century; and a *casus belli* (of course you have been brushing up your Latin) was found in the fact, and I wish you to note this particularly, that the Turks ill-treated the Christians of the Greek Church within the Sultan's dominions.   You perceive the application of the story of the wolf and the lamb here,

don't you?" The youth gave a knowing bow.
"Well," pursued Kwamankra, "it is a long
story; but, in the act of self-preservation by the
Turks, although history recordeth it not in so
many words, the circumstance constituted in the
minds of the Russians of the time a 'Muslim
peril,' do you understand?"

"Yes, dad," answered the youth eagerly.
"But, surely, the English people have never acted
thus toward a weaker race. I can well understand the sneaking bear thus acting, but not
straightforward John Bull."

"Well, let us see, I am not so sure about that.
What of the Opium War with China when
England coerced China because she insisted upon
restricting the sale of opium within the Chinese
Empire, and the 'Lorcha Arrow' incident not so
many generations ago, where England picked a
quarrel with China, because Governor Yen exer-
cised the right of boarding a Chinese vessel which
wrongly flew an English flag to cover her piratical
practices in Chinese waters? Other instances
might be given, but I can assure you, my dear
boy, no Christian European nation is free
from the error of self-assertiveness—none free
from the taunt of crying 'yellow peril,' or 'black
peril,' the moment they are confronted with
resistance in one form or another. They seem to
carry in the one hand a patent from the Almighty

and absolution in the other to snatch away the patrimony of others :

' Why should they live—Fate has writ large its doom for them.
' Land for the whites ! Let the black fellows die ! '

the European nations seem to shout, and reck not offence to God or man in the cry."

" But how does all this apply to our country ? " asked Ekra Kwow.

" How does it ?—good ! I like to think you are following so closely what the learned books call the argument, that is, the immediate subject under discussion. Well, I will tell you in one word. The Political Officer represents the self-assertiveness of the English in extending power and authority at every nook and corner wherever the thin end of the wedge can be introduced. The sagacious black man offers a point of resistance when he pleads his peculiar customs and institutions, and presto ! the cry of the ' educated native peril ' is raised, as if forsooth, the ' native ' ceases to be a ' native ' the moment he is educated. The genuine cry might be ' the black peril,' but that won't do at present. The wolf and the lamb story again, you see."

" But why don't you expose these things, dad ? You can write, you can talk, why don't you let the whole world know of them," said the lad with some degree of heat.

"Not so fast, my boy," said Kwamankra, laying his hand on the child's head, and speaking slowly and deliberately, as was his wont when about to give vent to some utterance from the very recesses of his soul. " I wish you to understand, my dear child, that it is neither the anger of the powerful, nor the hope of favour from the great that has hitherto sealed my lips. I have taught you from your infancy to regard truth as the highest of all virtues, as the apex of character; and he who falls in declaring the truth in his day and generation, is but a humble follower of a Socrates, or if you prefer it, of the Nazarene. I try to follow his example, prepared to suffer if needs be in the cause of country, race, and humanity," and drawing the child nearer, he added in suppressed tones—" only the hour is not yet come. Pray for thy father, that when it does come, he may be found strong and faithful."

CHAPTER XI.

ON "THE GREAT NORTH WESTERN."

CHAPTER XI.

On " The Great North Western."

" I say, boys, what class are you travelling," shouted Aban to Tandor-Kuma and Kwamankra.

" I go neither first nor second," returned Tandor-Kuma; and as the Gold Coast Government Railway boasts of only two classes, Kwamankra said, " Look here, you fellows, I am a man of peace. If you are going to have any larks, I would rather take the down train twenty-four hours hence."

By this time the bell announcing the hour for the departure of the train had sounded. So Kwamankra rushed to secure a first-class ticket, leaving the " Professor " and Tandor-Kuma to their own devices. When he returned, the two had occupied seats in the first-class compartment and started to make themselves merry with the good things which Kwamankra had provided for the journey.

" Here's to you and another five hundred a year, as the chaps over the water say "—this as the " Professor " raised his glass in the direction of Kwamankra. Seeing there was no alternative,

I

the latter resigned himself to the situation, and good-humouredly toasted the company round.

"Teekets! teekeets!" shouted the collector from the second-class end of the "composite carriage." Of course, you know what a "composite carriage" is? If you don't, I will enlighten you. It is the kind of thing on this particular railway in which the whites travel at one end, their servants and the black élite at the other end, while the ordinary blacks are packed like sardines in a detached carriage, labelled "second-class." Not that there is any rule prohibiting black gentlemen from using a first-class carriage, but the fact is the class referred to know better, and have too much self-respect to travel first, except on rare occasions when they can have a carriage all to themselves.

To resume, "teekeets! teekeets!" sounded nearer. By this time the "Professor" was in the middle of a Mississippi story, and his brush with buffaloes and other hair-breadth escapes. After taking a cheap degree, with his usual erratic disposition, Aban had been travelling, often supporting himself by odd jobs, and had included in his experiences an acquaintance with the Japs of whom he was never tired of speaking. The ticket collector eyed the three black gentlemen furtively once or twice, and seemed to have come to a mental resolve not to disturb them for the nonce, nor did the trio disturb him by so much as a momentary notice of his presence.

Just as he was about retreating to the second-class compartment, Kwamankra shouted after him, " I say, collector, won't you have a drink? " holding out to him some whisky and soda—" the others do it, you know," and this with a knowing wink.

The collector was human. He hesitated, then made up his mind, took the drink, and went away. Presently he returned and became communicative.

" I don't know, Sar, if any of you, Sar, be lawyer man, Sar? "

Tandor-Kuma chuckled. " What next," demanded the "Professor" sternly. Kwamankra held his peace, appearing not to listen.

" I don't know, Sar, but I bin tink say I da go show you di rules which say di collector mus examin ebery gentman him teekeet."

Kwamankra began to fumble in his pockets. " My good man," said the " Professor " to the collector, " I have made it a rule never to give up my ticket on *this* line till I have landed safely at my destination, do you understand? "

The emphasis seemed to upset the equilibrium of the collector. He sneaked away, may be, to reflect upon the advantage of an emphasis, and sure enough, he was soon heard letting off steam in the second-class compartment at the expense of an inoffensive Fanti.   I 2

By this time the train had passed Mansu. Shortly after leaving that station there was some trouble with one of the vans getting off the rails; and it was a matter of half-an-hour before it was set right. Half-way between Mansu and Ashieme, some timber was taken, and as they steamed away in the twilight, the train with its composite appendages was a full furlong long! Soon they were in thick darkness.

"Light, collector, light!"—this from Kwamankra, for in the detached carriage could be heard yells and shrieks of women and children.

"I say, collector, light! Do you hear? Light!" and this with an expletive or two from the "Professor." The expletive did its work. The collector made his way to the composite carriage amid a scene of much confusion.

"You had better go and fetch the Inspector to see about this mess, or I will report the whole lot of you fellows, white and black alike. It is perfectly disgraceful, this kind of thing," said Tandor-Kuma.

The Inspector, who had, in the meantime, been hurried to the detached compartment by the shrieks of the women and children, had by this time got into the composite carriage.

"What the deuce are you doing not having yet lighted the carriage," he said to the collector with an offended air.

" I no get mach, Sar! Railway no buy me
mach, Sar!"

The Inspector made as if he would knock the
collector down, but thought better of the matter,
and, snatching a borrowed match box, quickly
tried to light the lamp. Puff! went out the light.

" Try again, Sir," suggested Kwamankra dryly.
" There may be a drop of water in the oil." Puff!
went out the light the second time.

" Try again! try again!" came from all sides.
" Shall I get out and buy you some paraffin, Mr.
Inspector? You know this is perfectly disgraceful. Thirteen shillings for thirty-nine miles and
no oil," said Tandor-Kuma.

" Try again! try again! knock him down, teach
him a lesson," shouted some roughs. It was
getting a bit exciting. The Inspector beat a hasty
retreat.

" They call dis di Govmont railway. It is di
dirtiest hole I have been in. South Africa, East
Africa, North Africa, they be countries. Dis
country is disgraceful to the British Govmont,"
put in a Frenchman at the corner.

Pu! pu! pu! piyu!! Pu! pu! piyu!! came the
heartbreaking snort from the nostrils of the iron
horse. It reminded one of an overworked omnibus
horse at midnight in Oxford Street. First back-
wards, then downwards, up the incline, and down
the gradient, toyed the iron horse, and as Tandor-

Kuma thought of his wife and children waiting dinner in the cosy little room across the bridge, he could not help inwardly bestowing a blessing upon the devil and all his works. It was not until 9.30 p.m. that the terminus was made, the party having left on their 39 miles run at 2.30 p.m. As the trio walked the lonely streets, where black men are scarcely seen after sunset, the Professor, as a parting reminder, said to Kwamankra, " On principle I never pay for a ticket on this line until I have made the terminus, and if you are a wise man, you will take my tip."

CHAPTER XII.

A LEADER OF SOCIETY.

TOM PALMER, the son of Jonathan Palmer, of Horse Road, Ussher Town, Accra, was a goodly youth of many fine qualities. The Palmers originally hailed from Sierra Leone, settling on the Gold Coast early in the fifties of the last century. By dint of great energy, combined with uncommon business tact, the first Palmer had gradually won for himself a competence which the second Palmer, with equal tact, had gone on improving, so that when it came to the turn of Jonathan Palmer, he was looked up to as a man of wealth, position, and influence in the community of Accra.

Jonathan Palmer had contented himself with money making, but his son and heir, the goodly Tom Palmer, had combined book-learning with his other accomplishments, and gone to the extent of taking the L.Th. degree at the College in Freetown, though he never had the intention of entering the Church. He was fond of controversy, and as the L.Th. course combined a certain amount of historical information, he had followed it so as to be able to hold his own against all comers, as he pugilistically put it. For a calling he had chosen agriculture, and was an expert in the secrets of soils, manures, and seasons. Not that he practised agriculture, as men practise medicine for example. Oh, dear no! He was a dilettante and no more. It was enough for him to be able to say with truth, I am a scientific agriculturist, and I can give you a point or two. Besides, in a community like Accra, where every respectable citizen has a calling, it would not have done to appear a loafer.

Tom Palmer was an ambitious youth. His aim in life was to be the leader of society in the community where it had pleased Providence to place his father and his father's father before him. His was the family fortune by right after the pater was gone. He would be the leader of the black aristocracy. What was there to prevent it? And, so, he set to work with a will. The cut of his coat was always up to date, and, on the Sabbath, he studiously appeared in church in a silk hat and patent leather boots, and never forgot his button-hole and gloves of approved style, though he was never guilty of the solecism of wearing the latter by reason of the tropical temperature. For the same reason also he generally wore his coat sleeves a little turned up, so as to show plenty of linen, and the tips of his trousers followed suit, so that you could count the white buttons on his boots. Other youths of his generation looked on admiringly—looked on, and pined, and strove to be like him in appearance, and many succeeded, though they had not Tom Palmer's culture, for which his early associations were responsible or his money.

Freetown is an advanced African community. Notwithstanding the fact that some, not having the fear of God in their hearts, have thought it fit to malign her in print, still the reader may take it from the writer that it is a community that has nothing to be ashamed of. It has produced many a distinguished citizen, remarkable alike for intellectual attainments as for business enterprise and success, so much so, that Her late Majesty had thought it not amiss to bestow the honour of knighthood upon one of her esteemed sons. Besides, the city boasts of a cathedral, a rarity in the West African Dependencies. The singing is one of the finest on the West Coast, and men like Canon Spain, Canon Wilson, and Canon Moore, all black clerics, would do honour to any English See. It was no wonder, therefore, that Tom Palmer was truly proud of his *Alma Mater*, the Fourah Bay College, duly affiliated to Durham University, and of the City of Freetown, the Mecca of West Africa. Truly, if there was one thing more than another

for which Tom Palmer revered the memory of his
paternal grandfather, it was the utter unselfish-
ness with which he had transmitted the savings of
his father before him to his son Jonathan, and
the likelihood of the latter obeying the paternal
injunction to transmit, in his turn, the family
fortune to the next generation, that is, to him,
Tom Palmer. Yet, for all that, he could not
quite forgive his great forebear for quitting the
thriving community by the banks of the Roquelle
at the time he did.

With all the lightness of manner we have seen
in the subject of this sketch, yet must it be placed
to his credit that he was generally most careful
when taking any important step in life; and to
all the vexed questions in West African social life,
perhaps to none had he given such close study as
the marriage one. For, mark you, Tom Palmer's
aim in life was to be the leader of society, the
wankora wonkor, as a Fanti would say, in social
life at headquarters. Yet he could not make up
his mind somehow to do the thing. He had dis-
cussed the matter several times with friends
without ever coming to a satisfactory issue, and it
was, therefore, with particular relish that in
conversation with Kwamankra one day, who was
at Accra about this time for the Agricultural
Show, he managed to introduce his favourite
theme. Nor can we blame him. Every young

man contemplating marriage does it. He worries everyone he meets upon the subject upon the slightest encouragement, until finally he makes a fool of himself, or escapes by the skin of his teeth.

* * * * *

With an old world complaint upon her lips, the master philosopher met the complainant with the hint that one thing, after all, was essential. We all know the story, but some have, perhaps, not noted the human side of it. The complainant was plainly jealous of the marked attention the master philosopher paid to the younger sister. Her womanly instinct told her that the latter was fast discovering "the one thing needful." Her self-love asserted itself in the request, "Bid her that she help me." A charwoman's aid would have been as good. But, truth to tell, she would herself sit at the great man's feet, if she only knew how. It may be, thoughts like these were passing through Kwamankra's mind, as he slowly repeated more to himself than to his companion, the words of the teacher : "But one thing is needful! " then somewhat abruptly turning to the young man he said, " You are making the same mistake that most of us have made. We seem to think that love only comes when she is wooed in Parisian skirts and Regent Street high heels. Know then, my friend, that spiritual sympathy, like the wind, comes we know not whence. Happy the discerning ones who recognise the Queen of Heaven in whatever guise she approaches the waiting soul."

The young man was puzzled. He spoke his thoughts aloud. "What has all this to do with what I heard you muttering about the one thing needful?"

"What to do with it? I should think it has all to do with it," said Kwamankra gravely. "You have read the story, I daresay. The master finds a haven, a restful place, in the home of this particular family. Sympathy springs up between him and her who loved to sit at his feet, drinking in, as a thirsty soul, every word that fell from his lips. Interpret the master's sentiment as you may. But there is no need to disguise the fact that Mary had found the secret of life."

"But then, all this is beside the question, if you will permit me to say so. The sympathy between Christ and Mary was a thing apart, a spiritual relationship, if I may so put it. How can you talk of it in the same breath with mundane matters—with the vulgar thing which men profess and affect," said Tom Palmer, warming up to the subject in a way that interested his companion greatly.

Kwamankra eyed the young man for a second or two, and then said with a slight tremor in his voice, "If Jesus was not truly mundane, he would have no interest for you and me. Besides, if you

knew of the gift of the gods, you would not speak
of love in the way you have done. At one time I
was of like mind as you are, but riper experience
has taught me that there is nothing vulgar in
love, and that the feeling, in whatever guise it
exhibits itself, will be found, in its last analysis,
to be the self-same thing, and remember then, that
where love is, there God is. Great love, great
soul! As the streams flow into the rivers, and
the rivers into the sea, and yet the sea is not full,
even so does universal sympathy, from the cooing
of the dove to the fervent heat of a Romeo, find its
diapason in the God of Love.''

" I must confess," said the young man, " that
this way of looking at the matter is altogether new
to me. But am I to understand that you would
find excuse for the kind of sympathy that flies off
at a tangent here, there, and everywhere?''

" I will state you a stranger proposition then,''
said Kwamankra quietly. " Remember, my
young friend, to begin with, that love is a spiritual
magnetic force, and as I showed at the beginning
of our talk, like the wind it bloweth where it
listeth. Remember also that there are affinities
and repulsions where one might least expect.
Oftentimes one starts from the north pole, another
from the south, and the magnetic force draws
them on and on until they meet, and, in this sense,
are we the children of circumstances. Now, think

of it.   Here is a man of great magnetic force,
evoking sympathy and love wherever he goes.
But he is a mere man.   The corresponding force
which he attracts and calls into play here and
there becomes created entities, begging for life and
claiming the right to live.   Tell me, what is the
duty of the giver of this life, under God, or to
put it materially, the creator of this force?
Must he allow free scope to the play of sympathy,
or must be ruthlessly set to work to destroy the
hope of *light* which he bids spring up in a human
soul?''

"Again, I do not understand you, unless you
would imply nothing material in what you say.''

" I have said nothing that is difficult to understand,'' pursued Kwamankra.   " Bear in mind I
am speaking of true love.   I am not referring to
a mere wild senseless passion, the result of egoism,
the kind of thing which finds satisfaction in
multiplying wives, and, from that point of view,
I speak of things spiritual rather than material.
This, then, I say that no one who has the capacity
to evoke sympathy in the human soul has the right
ruthlessly to quench the fire once his flame has
kindled.   I will tell you a story, if you care to
listen.''

" Go on, please,'' said the young man.

" Well, here it is.   ' Once upon a time there
lived a youth who in the heyday of joyous inex-

perience, as he chanced by a certain out-of-the-way village, evoked love in the breast of a young damsel much below him in degree, and he wot not the full meaning of what he had done. The years rolled leisurely past, and her lover never returned. In the meanwhile, he had become great, gotten himself honour and riches, and, withal, love besides, as he thought. Now and again in the dim recesses of memory a recollection of the maiden would come back to him; but he would say, that is a thing of the past, let the dead past bury its dead. But, as obeying some irresistible impulse, day by day, the thought gained upon him. What was at first a mere curiosity to know what had become of her, grew in intensity until it ended in a regular quest. Abroad he bade his servants go, if, haply, some news might come of her for whom his soul panted. But no news came. At last he gave up hope, and seemed to take no delight in his goodly surroundings, nay, not even in his wife, nor in his children and his home. One day, outside the city gate, as he returned from a lonely walk, he saw walking towards him the self-same woman whom youthful inexperience turned not back to see. Their eyes met. They had both aged so. They had also suffered. She frankly put forth her hands. His touched hers. " At last ! " she exclaimed, " my woman's heart told me sooner or later we should meet again." " And mine has been long lonely without thee," he said. "Moreover, riper knowledge has taught me that in the kingdom of love, nothing is ever lost." ' "

The story ended, the teller paused for a second, and then added, "Maybe you will now see in a truer light the one thing needful which shall not be taken away from her."

*   *   *   *   *

" Now putting philosophy aside for the moment, I daresay you have flirted a little in your time," said Kwamankra, good-humouredly, then, with a mischievous twinkle, " and you may have a child, a poor nameless one, in some out-of-the-way corner of the world. You needn't be shy about it. All of us do do it, though not all of us are men enough to own it. Now, believe me, my friend, any child of Eve, who has deliberately become the mother of your child is worthy of your love, and to treat her as an outcast is to be unworthy of the name of a man. In this wise, we pagans are more Christ-like than so-called Christians. ' He that is without sin among you, let him first cast a stone at her. And again, He stooped down and wrote on the ground,' " he quoted somewhat irrelevantly, then continued : " In Africa, she is protected; she is a wife. Call it polygamy, if you like. In so-called Christian countries she is despised, a prostitute, a leper."

*   *   *   *   *

In the fullness of time, Tom Palmer got married. None of his wives sought to be a leader of society, and he was well content. He himself did not seem likely, now that he had come to his heritage, that he would fulfil the promise of his early ambition. In due course the little ones came —so gladsome their little black faces wherever they appeared, the fulfilment of the radiant love which gave them birth. And as the years rolled by, it was sure that his girls were growing up to be useful members of the community, for Tom Palmer had made up his mind that he would have no Parisian skirts or Regent Street high-heeled nonsense, as he bluntly put it, nor would he ever condescend to explain himself.

K

CHAPTER XIII.

REAPING THE WHIRLWIND.

CHAPTER XIII.

REAPING THE WHIRLWIND.

TANDOR-KUMA lay sick with malaria. The fast boat that should have borne him to the bosom of his family had come and gone. In his dreams he had been talking wildly, and asking when the boat would be in.

It was not without reason that his uppermost thoughts seemed to hover about the movements of the steamers. There was in this house where he lay stricken, as a nurse, the mother of his first child—the kind of child the world sneers at and elects to ignore, who, nevertheless thrives and prospers to the amazement of those who talk glibly of the inscrutable ways of Providence.

He had hoped that in the few days he had to spend upon the business which brought him down, he would be so occupied and pressed with engagements, that he could very well manage to evade meeting more than in a casual way the mother of his child. And now a fortnight must elapse

K 2

before he would be well enough to travel, and
during that time what was to happen?

It is an unpleasant truth that in the first flush
of the shame of the mother of his child, instead of
bearing up bravely and sharing the shame with
her, like the coward man that he was, he had gone
so far as to protest that he was not the father of
the child, and had allowed her alone to pass
through the valley of humiliation; but the God
whom she had wronged, according to the theologians, had not suffered her to be entirely crushed.
Meanwhile, Tandor-Kuma had succeeded in life,
mounted up steadily in his calling, been happily
married, and was a most respectable member of
society. To do him justice, he was absolutely true
to his wife, whom he loved, and never meant to be
otherwise. In fact the contrast between his early
escapades and his present constancy and devotion
to his family was the common talk of those who
had known him in early life.

And here was he, after all these years, confronted with the same forbidden fruit of his early
days. He was young and full of fire in those days,
it is true. He had fallen then. Was it likely he
could resist now that he began to feel the same old
witchery taking possession of his heart, and
making a fool of him, if not in deed, in very
intention? " O, God! " he cried, ardently and
sincerely, " save me from this." But even while

he cried, another voice within him said, "What does it matter? Is it your fault that you are stranded here?"

In the domestic arrangements of a West African home there is hardly any system; and so it happens that the master or mistress orders about the nearest hand available. This was a kind of hospital home. What was more natural than that Ekuba should gradually work her way to the bedside of him whom her heart adored? When the fever had abated a bit, now and again she would steal in with some daintily prepared refreshment which she would coax the patient to partake of. She would often stay to say a word and to smooth his pillows. On such occasions Tandor-Kuma would seem ill at ease, and appear as if struggling with some inward emotion.

Careful nursing had brought Tandor-Kuma back to health; but, as it sometimes happens in West Africa, the boat that was to take the convalescent home had not turned up according to the time-table, and time was hanging most painfully on his hands; and every day the Titan of sheer sympathy was tightening its grasp stronger and stronger round his heart, leaving his senses reeling.

One evening Ekuba came to clear away the supper and found Tandor-Kuma sitting at a corner of the room reading, the others having gone

to a Fanti concert.   She boldly drew a chair, and
sat down near him.

" What a jolly thing your steamer delaying
like this.   Supposing she did not come for another
week or so, I wonder whatever will happen? "
Tandor-Kuma raised up a finger deprecatingly.

" I know," continued Ekuba, not heeding the
warning one little bit, " that you are dying to get
back to the bosom of your dear family—that is
what they call it, isn't it?   But what must be,
must be."

" What do you mean, Ekuba, you talk rather
strangely to-night."

" I simply mean this, that I have missed you
badly all these years, and now that the spirits of
my fathers have thrown you in my way once more,
surely you will not begrudge me a little of your
society.   I took a job here with your kinsman, the
doctor, feeling sure you would one day turn up."

" Don't talk like that, Ekuba.   You know I
must be careful.   I am a married man, and I must
think of my wife and children."

" If it comes to that," she said, " I am your
first wife, and the second is an interloper."   So
saying, she burst out into a wild laugh.   The
situation was becoming perilous and yet comical,
and Tandor-Kuma could not restrain a laugh too.
Here he was with the woman, who first raised
sympathy in him, confronting him with a naïveté

that was quite unusual. Should he repulse her? He quickly decided that the wisest course was to humour her and talk the matter out in a half-bantering, half-serious way with her.

"You know," said Ekuba, taking advantage of a momentary pause on the part of Tandor-Kuma, "the last time you were here, and you had to go away so suddenly, when I came and found you were gone. I was so sorry," looking at Tandor-Kuma defiantly.

"Were you? I am not surprised. You see we all make mistakes in life, and we are expected to pull ourselves together and go straight after. If not, often the last stage is worse than the first. You don't wish to see me down, do you?"

"It depends upon what you mean by seeing you down. Kobina had to come, and nothing could prevent it; and I have waited all these years," repeating the last words with a slow emphasis and a weariness of tone which struck Tandor-Kuma awkwardly.

"If you talk like that, I shall never come to this place again, when I go away this time."

"It doesn't matter; I shall wait; and it may be some sudden business or family matter will bring you down."

Tandor-Kuma revolved in his mind how to meet this flank move. Meanwhile she continued: 'You know I go to chapel? Last night the minister told us in his address that, once upon a time, there was a king who was in the habit of killing his subjects for no good reason. One day he sent for a parson. The good man feared and wondered whatever was going to happen. He made excuses, but eventually had to go. While going he broke his leg. It took some days to set him right, and he was well enough to continue his journey. When he arrived at the king's palace, he was dead, and so the parson was saved." She stopped short, eyeing the man she loved feverishly.

"Well?" interrogated Tandor-Kuma.

"Well, simply this that what must be must be, and what must not be must not be—that is the rule of the gods"—pointing her little chin up triumphantly. "And after all," she went on, "was it such a grave error? You know the murderer was not saved, but the thief was."

"But what if the thief went on stealing," retorted Tandor-Kuma. "It is like going against the light."

"Light, then darkness," Ekuba put in with a far away look in her eyes.

"Yes, but when the light comes, then darkness goes away," suggested Tandor-Kuma.

It was all very fine, this toying with fine phrases and sentiments when passion answered to passion in the breasts of two human beings. Ekuba lapsed into silence, and it was evident that both man and woman were struggling with the same inward emotion.

"But tell me," Tandor-Kuma incautiously broke out, "what made you run away from me the last time I was here before I got married."

"How simple you men are? I ran away from you? It was not so. I simply went to avoid compromising you in any way."

Tandor-Kuma would have liked a little time to reflect. But suddenly Ekuba swept away the supper things, and, in a moment, she was gone.

The next morning, a gentle tap was heard at the door of Tandor-Kuma, and a voice from within said, "come in." Ekuba boldly entered, and placing down some clean linen, flung herself at Tandor-Kuma's feet, who was already dressed and reclining in a low chair by the open window. Tandor-Kuma got up and faced her.

"What is this you have done," he said under his breath, perceiving the awkwardness of the situation. For answer Ekuba got up and deliberately locked the door upon the outside world. Then facing the man, she said, "Tandor-Kuma, these many years my heart has hungered for your sympathy, and now that the gods have brought you back to me, surely, you will not deny me one kind word. Just say you care for me a little. That is all I want."

Tandor-Kuma made a move as if he would

unbolt the door. In that instant Ekuba held him spell-bound with a look so pitiful, so imploring, so passionate that he quailed before her gaze. He hesitated, then wavered. The next moment he completely broke down. Erring love had conquered, that was all.

CHAPTER XIV.

THE BLACK MAN'S BURDEN.

A BAMBOO shanty, doing service as a Methodist place of worship at the end of a " High Street," with a mud house roofed with corrugated iron, doing service for Bellal, with gin shops and sheds studded all along the line at short intervals at the other end—such is a typical scene in a well-known growing African community in the neighbourhood of the thriving mines on the Gold Coast railway. It is a terrible scourge, a veritable canker, eating its way slowly, yet surely, into the very vitals of the life of the black people among whom this plague of modern civilisation is planted.

It is the Christian Sabbath and the hour of morning service. Ding, dong! ding, dong! goes the bell, calling the devotional black folk of the community to worship. They are not inattentive to the call, if one may judge from the group after group of men, women, and children wending their way up the little rising on whose summit stands the House of God. The women far outnumber the men, and the house is filled to its utmost capacity. At a corner, all by himself, sits a son

of Albion, a man of independent character, the
butt of the camp, who dares to worship with the
black folk on this holy day.   It is a motley
gathering of all conditions of men in all sorts of
costumes from the latest Regent Street cutaway
coat to the ample four fathoms of Manchester
calico print, gracefully wound round the person.
At 10.30 of the clock there mounts the pulpit a
black parson who, from that hour till 11.50, reads
Psalms and Litanies and hymns to the melody of
an inharmonious portable American organ.   No
wonder half the congregation go to sleep, and the
beadles have their work cut out for the rest of the
morning.   One of their number, aggravated by the
extra rise in the thermometer, is a bit aggressive,
and no wonder that a distinct unchristian scowl
is clear on the face of a Christian gentleman
sitting next to the observer.

Meanwhile, the reverend seigneur is discoursing
in an unknown tongue to the majority of the congregation for all he is worth, and when he conde-
scends at length to render the sermon into the
vernacular, the finest Job-type in the congregation
is not listening, but wondering when this labyrinth
of a service will end.   In the meanwhile, what of
the house of Belial?

" Pretty polly! pretty polly! how do do? Quite
well, thank you, pretty polly! tut! tut! " are the
various sounds that attract the attention of the

wayfaring man from the throats of half-a-dozen tropical birds attached to the house of Belial. It is true the worshippers are but few and far between, mostly, and, in fact, nearly all, of one race. But their worship is real, sincere, and earnest. The black folk are beginning to understand and to appreciate that there is other worship than that of God, and that both are taught by the white man's fetish which they call civilisation.

But a livelier scene remains yet to be described. The inmates of the gin shops are issuing forth in their tens and larger groups. They dance and gesticulate, as if seized by some evil spirit, and the uproar is worthy the confusion and the clamour of the nether regions. That is also the white man's work.

And so it happens that the black man along the line is sorely pressed by a three-fold burden—the burden of allurement in the shape of gin drinking; allurement in the shape of houses of ill-fame; the bantering hypocrisy of the allurer. Heavens what curse is equal unto this curse!

Meanwhile, from the Moslem quarter of the village community at dawn, noon, and dusk goes forth the voice of the Muezzin, as from the minarets of Mecca, calling unto the faithful to prayer. They drink neither wine nor strong drinks, nor suffer them to come near their habitations the unclean thing. They keep alive their primitive

simplicity and faith, combining Godliness with
contentment. It is a struggle between the CROSS
and the CRESCENT. Which will win? It looks as
if the Crescent will win in the end, judging by
the Divine standard of life; and yet Christ is
stronger than Mahomet. But the House of Christ
is divided against itself, because the men of that
House, nay, the very leaders and the lamp bearers,
are untrue!

"Good evening, Sir," said a white miner to
Kwamankra. "Can you tell me where the West
Indian gentleman who plays the guitar lives?"

"Certainly; if you will step over here I will
show you," said Kwamankra, rising up from his
simple evening repast. "You know the market
place; if you will walk straight down and take the
first turning to your left, I believe you will find
him in the first house but one."

Kwamankra settled down to his meal, thankful
to have got rid of what threatened to be a serious
interruption to his thoughts.

In ten minutes the miner came back. "May I
come in?" he asked.

"Yes, do," replied Kwamankra.

"I did not find him; they say he has gone down
to the Coast. What is your name?" essayed the
miner; "you speak English so well. Are you a
lawyer?" He spoke a little thickly. Kwamankra
did not answer, but put on a whimsical look which

said as nearly as possible, " what if I am ? " at
the same time beckoning the miner to take a seat.

" You know I have seen you somewhere before.
Your face is familiar. It must have been on the
train," persisted the miner.

" Yes, I come up and down here pretty often."

" You know I came down to-night on purpose to
have a little fun with the photographer over the
way. I am good for a right down American sing-
song, and, if you don't mind, we can have a fine
time together."

" No, thank you, I have some writing work to
do, and I must be getting on before bedtime.
Kofi, please show this gentleman round to the
photographer's across the way "—addressing his
servant on the verandah.

" Oh, may I have a drink of water ? "

" I have some Tuborg beer, excellent stuff; perhaps you will find that pleasanter—Kofi, fetch
some beer." The miner subsided into the comfortable canvas chair round the corner.

" Well, Boss," he pursued, " I know of a little
job I can put in your way. There is a man in my
camp who has worked for one year and fourteen
days, and just because he had a little fun to-day,
he has been turned adrift, and he is to pay his
passage back home. Now, do you think that's
fair ? If you will take up the matter, I will send
him round in the morning. What name shall I

say?" The same quizzical look and a smile by way of encouragement to get on and be finished with the business was all the response Kwamankra gave.

Meanwhile, the miner drained his second glass of Tuborg beer. He grew more confiding. "You know," he said, "they want me up there to do a platelayer's work; but old B. insists upon paying me only fifteen bob a day, and, as I am no fool, I keep my ' sabi ' there," pointing significantly to his head. "Besides, they think I am too familiar with the black people, and when they see me sitting down and drinking with them, they don't like it; but I don't care. There is no part of this district I have not been to, and the Fantis have always behaved to me like gentlemen, and I am always ready to do them a good turn. You know old B. wanted to play me the same trick as my pal. He says to me the other day, ' You are drunk, and, if this occurs again, away you go bag and baggage.' Mind you, I wasn't drunk. To-day I got drunk, and I go up and says to him : ' Now, Mr. B., I am drunk, and very drunk too, and if you are a man come out in your shirt sleeves, and we shall have it out.' He was as tame as a lamb "—this almost in a whisper, accompanied by a low laugh. Kwamankra joined in it heartily.

"Kofi, show this gentleman the way to the photographer's—mind you, Sir, there are ditches in the way," said Kwamankra.

"Good-night, Sir," returned the miner. In another ten minutes he had returned. Kwamankra was busy with his scribbling. He hardly dared interrupt the flow of ideas.

"The photographer is out, I am told," explained the miner.

"Very good, Sir—good night," said Kwamankra, hardly looking up from his writing.

"As a last favour, would you mind showing me where I can find a bed for the night? I am told there is a hotel about here."

"I am sure I don't know of one, and I would advise you to get back to your camp," said Kwamankra, fixing a penetrating glance upon the miner, which said plainly, 'I wonder if you are an honest man.' With this the miner vanished into the outer darkness, but the story is silent the while whether the same operation was not repeated elsewhere that night.

The next day Kwamankra was due down the Coast, and he took the afternoon train with the "Professor" for a companion. The second-class compartment was full, so they travelled first, and though there were many angry glances, none dared question them. Kennedy Bilcox, the Political Officer, was also going down by the same train, and being minded to be gracious, and having had an extra parting glass more than was good for him, he was inclined to be confiding. Besides, though

L

he immensely disliked men of colour, he judged it
politic outwardly to be on the best of terms with
the leaders of the people.   He thought he gained
their confidence that way.   Rather he raised their
suspicions, and was accordingly mistrusted.

On this auspicious occasion, he was full of the
big things he had done up country—how he had
metaphorically thrashed the Chief of Tandosu
into humility, and how he crouched before him
with fear, poor man!   Presently he turned to
Kwamankra and said : '' I say, do you know that
rascal Kobina Bua?   I hear he is your client.
You had better advise him to behave properly in
future, or, by Jove, he will find himself at St.
Jago.''

'' But   what   has   he   done? ''   queried
Kwamankra.

'' What has he done?   Why the fool is perpetu-
ally drunk, has lost all sense of decency, and is
always making a ' palaver '' at Tandosu.''

'' Oh, is that all? '' said Kwamankra, pro-
vokingly.

'' You do surprise me, Mr. Kwamankra.   To
think that a man of your position and education
should see nothing to condemn in the disgraceful
conduct of Kobina Bua! ''

'' Personally I condemn no man, but since you
talk of condemnation, permit me to point out to
you that the greater condemnation lies at the door

of the Government whom you represent, and whose servant you are. You condemn Kobina Bua, and you presume to do so by reason of the fact that you are a Political Officer. As a fair-minded man, let me invite you to look at the other side of the picture. You know that trade gin contains fusel oil and other deadly noxious ingredients. You also know that that is the stuff the Government permit to be imported into the country and which eventually finds its way down the throats of 'rascals' like Kobina Bua. You dare not stop the importation of the vile stuff. Why! because it would affect salaries and pensions and duty allowances and other perquisites. In the name of reason, how can you expect the average black man having the means to indulge in gin drinking to keep his head and behave decently? And so when a Government Officer pays a visit to one of these otherwise harmless African dignitaries, and he is received by the latter with extra warmth, where-upon the Officer losing his self-control, vents upon him his wrath in eloquent periphrasis and damn-ing reports reach headquarters, the observer, if he is a seeker after truth, certainly feels tempted to tap the Officer lightly on the back and say : ' Thou hypocrite, first cast the beam out of thine eye, and then shalt thou see clearly to cast the mote out of thy brother's eye.' '' Kennedy Bilcox appeared thunderstruck, but Kwamankra, unheeding, continued : " You know, and the whole world knows, that if the black chief and his people stopped consuming the vile stuff the merchants offer them, the whole machinery of Government would stop running for want of the necessary grease. You are a Christian, of course. When you meet your friends, and, in conclave, you are inclined to be hard on my client, remind yourselves of the Master's saying : ' Ye make clean the outside of the cup and platter . . . ye tithe mint and rue and all manner of herbs and pass over judgment and the love of God.' "

* * * * *

As the Professor and Kwamankra shook hands at the station, the former said to his friend : " Those were brave words. But you may be sure this kind of thing will get you into trouble one of these days. But here's my hand on it, whenever you need help I am your man."

Kwamankra spoke low : " I have counted the cost, and, it may be, I shall need thy help when the hour comes."

CHAPTER XV.

AS IN A GLASS DARKLY.

NOT so very long ago in the age of the world, the Nations were gathered in council upon Mount Atlas, even at the point which is nearest the ancient city of Constantine, and there were no people that were not represented, save the Ethiopians, whose kingdoms stretch from the shores of the Mediterranean, where it washes the Lybian coast, across the great desert, taking in the arms of the mighty waste from ocean to ocean, thence sweeping down to the remotest parts of the provinces inhabited by the Kaffirs, a race of mighty men.

It was like the meeting of the gods, the gathering of the Nations, for they had mastered all knowledge and gotten themselves such power as to make men forget the Power beyond, before whom the Nations of the Earth are as grasshoppers.

These Nations, who, in the old pagan days, struggled the one against the other in true manly fashion, had learnt a new method of warfare, which they labelled '' Diplomacy ''; and when the uninitiated asked the reason for the change, it was explained that it was dictated by the spirit of their common religion which inculcated universal brotherhood, and the beating of swords into plough-shares. Wherefore it came to pass, that at this universal conference the Nations said smooth things to one another which no one believed.

But there was one thing concerning which these mighty men were in earnest, and that was the capture of the soul of Ethiopia. Said they, " We have all increased in knowledge and power, and, being brothers, we can no longer devour one another. Yet must we live. Taught by the instinct of self-preservation, we must have elbow-room wherein our children and our children's children may thrive. Now, before our hosts lieth the whole stretch of Ethiopia from sea to sea. Come, let us partition it among ourselves." They were well agreed upon this matter, but not upon the way of encompassing it.

One Nation said, " How shall we do this thing, seeing we are Christians?" Another said, " Thou that doubtest, thou art merely slow of counsel. This thing is easily done. We shall go to the Ethiopians, and shall teach them our religion, and that will make them ours, body and soul—lands, goods, and all, for all time." And the saying pleased them all.

It came to pass upon the third year after the meeting of the Nations that a mighty prince, sailing from the setting sun, dropped anchor in that portion of Ethiopia which is washed by the waters of the Gulf of Guinea. Retinue he had none, nor arms, nor any outward sign of power. In his hand he held a simple cross, and gifts besides. The Sons of Night gathered around him in great awe, and took the coming of the stranger for the visit of a god. But the gifts set them easy, and the drink of the white man was like nectar unto them.

There were discerning men among the Ethiopians who would shake their heads and say, This thing will bring us no good. But the crowd submitted to the worship of the new god, and greedily devoured the good things found upon his altars. And soon the discerning ones formed themselves into a group, and the crowd in another camp; and the thing pleased the strange visitor. And now he sent over the seas, and brought yet other teachers, who apparently taught the self-same doctrine, and the more they taught the more the people broke into smaller groups, each denouncing the other heartily. And so it came to pass, that children who had suckled at the same breast and had played with the same toy gods were, as men, feign to slay one another. And the thing seemed to please the new comers, and, being men of knowledge, they winked at one another and said the rest would follow.

By this time the unthinking crowd were beside themselves in emulation of the white man's ways, and when they bowed the knee in the House of Mammon, they thought they worshipped the true God, and seemed to forget that once they were Ethiopians.

*   *   *

The gods met in the ethereal heights of Mount Atlas to undo the work of mortals. Said they, '' The Nations are as a dream before us, and they know not what they do. Are not the Ethiopians a peculiar people, destined for a peculiar part in the world's work? An end to the machinations of men ! ''

In the self-same era a god descended upon earth to teach the Ethiopians anew the *way* of *life.* He came not in thunder, or with great sound, but in the garb of a humble teacher, a John the Baptist among his brethren, preaching racial and national salvation. From land to land, and from shore to shore, his message was the self-same one, which, interpreted in the language of the Christ, was : *What shall it profit a race if it shall gain the whole world and lose its own soul?*

CHAPTER XVI.

RACE EMANCIPATION—GENERAL CONSIDERATIONS : EDWARD WILMOT BLYDEN.

THE year 1907 found Kwamankra at Hampton, in the United States of America, as the guest of the African National University, which had been founded earlier in the century as the outcome of a spirit of intelligent co-operation on the part of the thinkers of the Ethiopian race both in the Mother Country and in their exiled home across the Atlantic. Gradually it had come to dawn upon educationists that the error of blindly imitating western methods must give place to original lines of racial intellectual development; and for that reason centres of learning were eager for information as to where mistakes had been made in the past, and how they might be remedied in the future.

Hampton has been described as one of the finest seats of learning in America. It is the work of Samuel Chapman Armstrong, a name which will ever be remembered with honour and veneration among cultured Ethiopians throughout the world, for it was left to him to point the way of freeing the souls of Africans in America after Abraham Lincoln and his stalwart men of iron will had freed their body.

It was "Emancipation Day," and the contrast between how the day was observed in earlier times on the plantations and the way the event was marked at Hampton on the occasion of Kwamankra's visit was extremely remarkable. The boisterous, rowdy, senseless jubilation of young and old had given way to a purposeful intent to mark each passing year with some record of national progress and efficiency; and it was inspiring to see the modest manner and the dignified calm of the students as they filed into the Chapel Theatre to the music of the University orchestra. But they had not long been seated when a low murmur could be heard all over the building which soon rose to a ringing cheer, as a side door opened, and the Principal of Hampton mounted the rostrum with Kwamankra and the professors following. Kwamankra had been announced to speak upon the work of Edward Wilmot Blyden, about the foremost thinker of the race, and great was the enthusiasm of the audience as with craned necks they took in every word of the speaker, as if it were a message from a new sphere. The speaker dwelt on the broader outlook which Dr. Blyden had, for at least forty years, presented to his countrymen in his writings which he passed under review, dwelling upon each distinctive note, and wound up in the following graphic words :—

" The claim of Edward Wilmot Blyden to the esteem and regard of all thinking Africans rests not so much upon the special work he has done for any particular people of the African race, as upon the general work he has done for the race as a whole.

" The work of men like Booker T. Washington and W. E. Burghart Du Bois is exclusive and provincial. The work of Edward Wilmot Blyden is universal, covering the entire race and the entire race problem.

" What do I mean? I mean this : that while Booker T. Washington seeks to promote the material advancement of the black man in the United States, and W. E. Burghart Du Bois his social enfranchisement amid surroundings and in an atmosphere uncongenial to racial development, Edward Wilmot Blyden has sought for more than a quarter of a century to reveal everywhere the African unto himself; to fix his attention upon original ideas and conceptions as to his place in the economy of the world; to point out to him his work as a race among the races of men; lastly, and most important of all, to lead him back unto self-respect. He has been the voice of one crying in the wilderness all these years, calling upon all

thinking Africans to go back to the rock whence
they were hewn by the common Father of the
nations—to drop metaphor, to learn to unlearn all
that foreign sophistry has encrusted upon the
intelligence of the African. Born in the West
Indies some seventy years ago and nurtured in
foreign culture, he has yet remained an African;
and to-day he is the greatest living exponent of
the true spirit of African nationality and manhood.

" To emphasise an important consideration, in
the Afro-American school of thought the black
man is seeking intellectually and materially to
show himself a man along the lines of progress of
the white man.   In the African school of thought,
represented by Dr. Blyden, the black man is
engaged upon a sublimer task, namely, the dis-
covery of his true place in creation upon natural
and national lines. That is the striking difference
between the two great schools of the thinkers of
the race.   And it has been the work of Edward
Wilmot Blyden to accentuate this difference, and
to-day he, of whom we are all so proud, is the
leading thinker of the latter school of thought.

" Apart from the magnetism of his personality,
the great influence of Dr. Blyden over the rising
thinking youth of the race, lies in the fact that he
has revealed in his writings and utterances the
true motive power which shall carry the race on

from victory unto victory. And all he has to say to his people, summing up his teaching in one word, is : man, know thyself.

" The voice that was aforetime crying solitarily in the wilderness has suddenly become the voice of a nation and of a people, calling unto their kindred across the Atlantic to come back to their way of thinking. We notice with a pang the strivings after the wind in which our brethren in America are engaged, and we ask them to-day to return to first principles and to original and racial conceptions—to those cooling streams by the fountains of Africa which would refresh their souls.

" To leave no possible doubt as to my meaning, ` Afro-Americans must bring themselves into touch with some of the general traditions and institutions of their ancestors, and, though sojourning in a strange land, endeavour to conserve the characteristics of the race. Thus and only thus, like Israel of old, will they be able, metaphorically, to walk out of Egypt in the near future with a great and a real spoil.

" Edward Wilmot Blyden is a leader among leaders of African aboriginal thought; and, lest a prophet should be without honour among his own kindred, I am happy on this occasion also to have, among others, the privilege and the opportunity of giving him the recognition that is his due."

For days and days the students of Hampton talked of little else besides the new conception of national aims presented in the address; and, in after years, it was noted that it gave a new colour and meaning to the good racial work done at Hampton.

CHAPTER XVII.

RACE EMANCIPATION—PARTICULAR
CONSIDERATIONS : AFRICAN NATIONALITY.

IN the name of African nationality the thinker would, through the medium of *Ethiopia Unbound,* greet members of the race everywhere throughout the world. Whether in the east, south, or west of the African Continent, or yet among the teeming millions of Ethiopia's sons in America, the cry of the African, in its last analysis, is for scope and freedom in the struggle for existence, and it would seem as if the care of the leaders of the race has been to discover those avenues of right and natural endeavour which would, in the end, ensure for the race due recognition of its individuality.

The race problem is probably most intense in the United States of America, but there are indications that on the African Continent itself it is fast assuming concrete form. Sir Arthur Lawley, the present Governor of Madras, before leaving the Governorship of the Transvaal, is reported in a public address to have said that the " black peril " is a reality, and to have advised the whites to con-

solidate their forces in presence of the potential
foe.   The leaders of the race have hitherto exer-
cised sound discretion and shown considerable
wisdom in advising the African to follow the line
of least resistance in meeting any combination of
forces against him.   The African's way to proper
recognition lies not at present so much in the
exhibition of material force and power, as in the
gentler art of persuasion by the logic of facts and
of achievements before which all reasonable men
must bow.

A two-fold danger threatens the African everywhere.   It is the outcome of certain economic conditions whose method is the exploitation of the
Ethiopian for all he is worth.   He is said to be
pressed into the service of man, in reality, the
service of the Caucasian.   That being so, he never
reaps the full meed of his work as a *man*.   He
materially contributes to the building of pavements on which he may not walk—take it as a
metaphor, or as a fact, which way you please.   He
helps to work up revenues and to fill up exchequers
over which, in most cases, he has no effective control, if any at all.   In brief, he is labelled as be-
longing to a class apart among the races, and any
attempt to rise above his station is terribly
resented by the aristocracy of the races.   Indeed,
he is reminded at every turn that he is only
intended to be a hewer of wood and a drawer of

water. And so it happens that those among the favoured sons of men who occasionally consider the lot of the Ethiopian are met with jeers and taunts. Is it any wonder, then, that even in the Twentieth Century, the African finds it terribly difficult to make headway even in his own country? The African may turn socialist, may preach and cry for reform until the day of judgment; but the experience of mankind shows this, that reform never comes to a class or a people unless and until those concerned have worked out their own salvation. And the lesson we have yet to learn is that we cannot depart from Nature's way and hope for real success.

And yet, it would seem as if in some notable instances the black man is bent upon following the line of greatest resistance in coping with the difficulties before him. Knowledge is the common property of mankind, and the philosophy which seeks for the Ethiopian the highest culture and efficiency in industrial and technical training is a sound one. It is well to arrest in favour of the race public opinion as to its capability in this direction. But that is not all, since there are certain distinctive qualities of race, of country, and of peoples which cannot be ignored without detriment to the particular race, country, or people. Knowledge, deprived of the assimilating element which makes it natural to the one taught,

M

renders that person but a bare imitator. The Japanese, adopting and assimilating Western culture, of necessity commands the respect of Western nations, because there is something distinctly Eastern about him. He commands, to begin with, the uses of his native tongue, and has a literature of his own, enriched by translations from standard authors of other lands. He respects the institutions and customs of his ancestors, and there is an intelligent past which inspires him. He does not discard his national costume, and if, now and again, he dons Western attire, he does so as a matter of convenience, much as the Scotch, across the border, puts away, when the occasion demands it, his Highland costume. It is not the fault of the black man in America, for example, that he suffers to-day from the effects of a wrong that was inflicted upon him years ago by the forefathers of the very ones who now despise him. But he can see to it that as the years go by it becomes a matter of necessity for the American whites to respect and admire his manhood; and the surest way to the one or the other lies not so much in imitation as in originality and natural initiative. Not only must the Ethiopian acquire proficiency in the arts and sciences, in technical and industrial training, but he must pursue a course of scientific enquiry which would reveal to him the good things of the treasure house of his own nationality.

There are probably but a few men of African descent in America who, if they took the trouble by dipping into family tradition, would not be able to trace their connection and relationship with one or other of the great tribes of West Africa; and now that careful enquiry has shown that the institutions of the Aborigines of Africa are capable of scientific handling, what would be easier than for the great centres of culture and learning in the hands of Africans in the United States to found professorships in this relation? In the order of Providence, some of our brethren aforetime were suffered to be enslaved in America for a wise purpose. That event in the history of the race has made it possible for the speedier dissemination and adoption of the better part of Western culture; and to-day Afric's sons in the East and in the West can do peculiar service unto one another in the common cause of uplifting Ethiopia and placing her upon her feet among the nations. The East, for example, can take lessons from the West in the adoption of a sound educational policy, the kind of industrial and technical training which would enable aboriginals to make the best use of their lands and natural resources. And, surely, the West ought not to be averse to taking hints from the East as regards the preservation of national institutions, and the adoption of distinctive garbs and names, much as

M 2

obtains among our friends the Japanese. While a student in London, a thrill of Oriental pride used to run through the writer when he brushed against an Asiatic in a garb distinctively Eastern. They aped no one. They were content to remain Eastern. For even when climatic conditions necessitated the adoption of European habiliments, they had sense enough to preserve some symbol of nationality. On the contrary, Africans would seem never to be content unless and until they make it possible for the European to write of them thus :

" How extraordinary is the spectacle of this huge race —millions of men—without land or language of their own, without traditions of the country they came from, bearing the very names of the men that enslaved them!

. . .

" The black element is one which cannot be ' boiled down ' into the great cosmopolitan American nation—the black man must always be tragically apart from the white man "—

and so on and so forth

Now, if there is aught in the foregoing which is true to life, it bears but one meaning, namely, this, that the average Afro-American citizen of the United States has lost absolute touch with the past of his race, and is helplessly and hopelessly groping in the dark for affinities that are not natural, and for effects for which there are neither national nor natural causes. That being so, the

African in America is in a worse plight than the Hebrew in Egypt. The one preserved his language, his manners and customs, his religion and household gods; the other has committed national suicide, and at present it seems as if the dry bones of the vision have no life in them. Looking at the matter closely, it is not so much *Afro-Americans* that we want as *Africans* or *Ethiopians*, sojourning in a strange land, who, out of a full heart and a full knowledge can say : If I forget thee, Ethiopia, let my right hand forget its cunning ! Let us look at the other side of the picture. How extraordinary would be the spectacle of this huge Ethiopian race—some millions of men—having imbibed all that is best in Western culture in the land of their oppressors, yet remaining true to racial instincts and inspiration, customs and institutions, much as did the Israelites of old in captivity ! When this more pleasant picture will have become possible of realisation, then, and only then, will it be possible for our people in bondage " metaphorically to walk out of Egypt in the near future with a great and a real spoil."

Someone may say, but, surely, you don't mean to suggest that questions of dress and habits of life matter in the least. I reply emphatically, they do. They go to the root of the Ethiopian's self-respect. Without servile imitation of our teachers in their get-up and manner of life, it stands to reason that the average white man would regard the average black man far more seriously than he does at present. The adoption of a distinctive dress for the cultured African, therefore, would be a distinct step forward, and a gain to the cause of Ethiopian progress and advancement. Pray listen to the greatest authority on national life upon this matter, " Behold, I have taught you statutes and judgments even as the Lord God commanded me that ye should do in the land whither ye go to possess it. Keep, therefore, and do them : for this is your wisdom and your understanding in the sight of the nations which shall hear these statutes and say, surely, this great nation is a wise and understanding people." Yes, my people are pursuing knowledge as for a hidden treasure, and have neglected wisdom and true understanding, and hence are they daily a laughing stock in the sight of the nations.

Here, then, is work for cultured West Africans to start a reform which will be world-wide in its effects among Ethiopians, remembering as a basis that we, as a people, have our own statutes, the customs and institutions of our fore-fathers, which we cannot neglect and live. We on the Gold Coast are making a huge effort in this direction, and though European habits will die hard with some of our people, the effort is worth making;

and, if we don't succeed quite with this generation, we shall succeed with the next. That the
movement is gaining ground may well be gathered
from the following extract from the *Gold Coast
Leader* of 24th February, 1907, reporting the
coronation of Ababio IV., *Mantse*, that is King,
of "British Accra." Says the correspondent :
" For the first time I realised that the Gold Coast
would be more exhilirating and enjoyable indeed
if the educated inhabitants in it would hark back
to the times of old and take a few lessons in the
art and grace of the sartorial simplicity and
elegance of their forebears. The 'scholars' looked
quite noble and full of dignity in the native dress.
There was not one ignoble or mean person among
them, and so for the matter of that did the ladies."

Then I should like to see *Ethiopian Leagues*
formed throughout the United States much in the
same way as the *Gaelic League* in Ireland for the
purpose of studying and employing Fanti, Yoruba,
Hausa, or other standard African language, in
daily use. The idea may seem extraordinary on
the first view, but if you are inclined to regard it
thus, I can only point to the examples of Ireland
and Denmark, who have found the vehicle of a
national language much the safest and most
natural way of national conservancy and evolution. If the Dane and Irish find it expedient in
Europe, surely the matter is worthy of considera-

tion by the Ethiopian in the United States, in
Sierra Leone, in the West Indies, and in Liberia.

A distinguished writer, dwelling upon the
advantages of culture in a people's own language
said : " These are important considerations of a
highly practical kind. Ten years ago, we had in
Ireland a people divorced, by half a century of
education conducted along alien lines, from their
own proper language and culture. We had also
in Ireland a people seemingly incapable of rational
action, sunk in hopeless poverty, apparently
doomed to disappear. We have in Ireland to-day
the beginnings of a system of education in the
national language and along national lines; and
we have at the same time, and in the places where
this kind of education has been operative, an
unmistakable advance in intellectual capacity and
material prosperity." Now, if the soul that is in
the Ethiopian, even in the United States, remains
Ethiopian, which it does, to judge from the coon
songs which have enriched the sentiment of mankind by their pathos, then, I say, the foregoing
words, true as everyone must admit they are, point
distinctly to the impossibility of departing from
nature's way with any hope of lasting good to
African nationality. I do sincerely trust these
thoughts will catch the eye of such distinguished
educationists as Mr. Booker T. Washington and
others of the United States and in the West Indies

as also the attention of similar workers in West Africa who have the materials ready at hand. It is a great work, but I do believe that my countrymen have the heart and the intelligence to grapple with it successfully.

CHAPTER XVIII.

RACE EMANCIPATION: THE CRUX OF THE MATTER.

CHAPTER XVIII.

RACE EMANCIPATION : THE CRUX OF THE MATTER.

ONE of the most pathetic passages in the history of human thought is the remarkable work of an Ethiopian, " The Souls of Black Folk," written by the well-known thinker, W. E. B. Du Bois, of Atlanta, Ga., in the United States of America. It deals with a matter which has attracted the attention of all thinking men of modern times. European writers have dealt with the question, and so have African and American writers. But the particular standpoint of Mr. Du Bois is peculiar unto itself. It recalls the story of the Hebrew people; but neither at the stage of actual enslavement, nor yet at the hour of emancipation. As yet, the people are roaming aimlessly in the wilderness, and the leaders, though having the promise, have but a glimmer of light to see distantly a day of deliverance possible. It is true twenty, thirty, years of the forty are past, and the full light may break some day all of a sudden; but even now the mighty arms of Moses must be upraised and supported lest the chosen people perish by the way.

It has been said that Mr. Du Bois' attitude toward the race question is a pathetic one. " I am a problem," our author would seem to say. Then presently follows the plaintive query : " How does it feel to be a problem ? " To descend to particulars, he says : " After the Egyptian and Indian, the Greek and Roman, the Teuton and Mongolian, the Negro is a sort of seventh son, born with a veil, and gifted with second sight in this American world—a world which yields him no true self-consciousness, but only lets him see himself through the revelation of the other world. It is a peculiar sensation, this double consciousness, this sense of always looking at one's self through the eyes of others, of measuring one's soul by the tape of a world that looks on in amused contempt and pity. One ever feels his twoness—an American, a Negro; two souls, two thoughts, two unreconciled strivings; two warring ideals in one dark body, whose dogged strength alone keeps it from being torn asunder." Ah ! there's the rub ! Poor Ethiopia ! how sorely hath the iron of oppression entered into the very soul of thy erring children !

Now, self-consciousness obviously depends upon self-revelation after which comes self-realisation. But has the Ethiopian sojourning in America, and, for that matter, even in Liberia and in Sierra Leone ever realised himself ? Has he received that self-awakening which would move him, in the words of the prodigal, to exclaim, "Alas me! How many hired servants of my father's have bread enough and to spare and I perish with hunger?" No, it has not yet occurred to him to arise and go to his Father, regardless of the taunts of the surly elder son. He perceives not yet that the Father is waiting to make a feast of rejoicing over the emancipation of his soul. No, he will not yet don the robe of sonship, nor suffer the ring, the symbol of a spiritual union and equality, to be placed upon his finger. Poor man! Instead of the fatted calf, he still sits sulkily by the wayside over Jordan apples which presently turn into ashes in his mouth. Listen to his cry: "Who shall deliver me from the burden of these unreconciled and irreconcilable strivings?" Listen! Not so long as he turns away from the Father's house and elects to remain a slave in soul. To be a puzzle unto others is not to be a puzzle unto one's self. The sphinx in the Temple of the Sphinx in ancient Egypt is a recumbent figure with the head of a lion, but with the features of King Chephron, the Master of Egypt, somewhere about 3960 B.C. Now, fancy Candace, Queen of Ethiopia, or Chephron, the Master of Egypt, being troubled with a double consciousness. Watch that symbolic, reposeful figure yonder, and you can but see one soul, one ideal, one striving,

one line of a natural, rational progress.   Look
again, and you must agree that the idea of a double
consciousness is absurd with these representative
types.   It is true that—

> " Bowed by the weight of centuries, he leans
> Upon his hoe and gazes on the ground;
> The emptiness of ages in his face,
> And on his back the burden of the world."

But, surely, to bear the burden of others, one
should have thought, is honourable work, and the
toiling one need not be a problem unto himself.

It is apparent that Mr. Du Bois writes from an
American standpoint, surrounded by an American
atmosphere.   And, of course, it is not his fault,
for he knows of no other.   To be born an African
in America, in that great commonwealth of dollars
and the merciless aggrandisement of the individual, where the weak must look out for himself,
and the cry of the innocent appeals not to him who
rides triumphantly to fortune, is to be entangled
in conditions which give no room for the assertion
of the highest manhood.   African manhood
demands that the Ethiopian should seek not his
opportunity, or ask for elbow room, from the white
man, but that he should create the one or the other
for himself.

Thoughts like these were stirring men's minds
when the Pan-African Conference met in the Gold
Coast in the year 1905, at the invitation of the

Gold Coast Aborigines Rights Protection Society, that prototype of the kind of African National Assemblies which must be called into being in the near future for the solution of African questions. Among the distinguished speakers at the Conference was Kwamankra, and great was the impression which was created by the paper which he read upon Dr. Blyden's great work upon " African Life and Customs," which is here recorded. Said he :

" I have followed, with keen interest, the series of articles on ' African Life and Customs ' in the *Sierra Leone Weekly News* from the ever instructive pen of Dr. Blyden ; and, perhaps, the following thoughts, suggested by them, may be useful to the student of African problems, seeking for the conditions suitable for Race Emancipation.

" I believe it was the learned doctor who first pointed out that Africa needs no redemption. But that she requires emancipation from the thraldom of foreign ideas inimical to racial development, few will doubt. What, indeed, can be more certain than that the African in the United States, in the West Indies, and in the mother country, East, West and South, has need to unlearn a good deal? But the unfortunate part of it is that the way out is at yet but dimly dawning even upon such as would otherwise be qualified to lead the masses. It becomes, therefore, the sacred duty of those who can see a little more clearly ahead to point the way. Hence it is that, in season and out of season, the warning voice of our grand old man is heard.

" The African who comes to his brethren with a red-hot civilisation straight from Regent Circus, or the Boulevards of Paris, and cries anathema to all black folk who would not adopt his views or mode of life, is, perhaps, not the man who is, or can be, of much help in developing African life and African idiosyncracies along the line of natural and healthy development. That is, perhaps, the underlying teaching, if not the sum total of the teaching, of the series of articles now before us.

" Africa seems destined for ever to be a land of mystery. When, in our modern way, we have demolished African strongholds, and, with the wantonness of an iconoclast, saved nothing to remind us of the artistic past and future possibilities of the people—nay, when we have laid out streets and encouraged shops to spring up mushroom-like here and there, we think we have solved the mystery of the gods, while, all the time, the heart of the matter is not reached. In many a forest glen they dwell in their tens and in their hundreds, but seldom in their thousands, undisturbed by the vulgar eye. Your cities are not their cities, your tinsel is not their gold. All they ask for is for as little interference as possible. What can you do with such a people, except to give them scope and room for natural development?

" I am writing this on the verandah of a house in the main street of Kumasi. Where once stood the palace of the King, now stands an ugly coast building with dirty blinds and a dirtier shop below. But the men and the women are not changed. The type is pronounced; and as I watch them passing up and down in different groups, it is easy to see that the men and women, who walked the banks of the Nile in days of yore, are not far different from the remnants of the sons of *Efua Kobi*. As you see the new unfinished coast houses side by side of the frail impermanent, quadrangular compounds of the old type, the thought suggests itself to you that, after all, it is the intangible that matters. You see you enter one of these compounds, and you find but bare, open rooms, in the case of a Chief's house, often supported by pillars. Where do these people actually live? Where do they keep their treasures, and their household gods? No one can tell you. But they are as safe as the golden stool itself is. Thus you arrive at the heart of these people, and you are inwardly persuaded that all the symbols of European authority, responsibility, and opportunity are more impermanent than the frail houses you see about you. How to reach the

N

heart of such a people would not be an uninteresting study. If you succeed, you have arrived at the heart of the principle which may be safely applied to healthy race development wheresoever necessary.

" Once more, then, Ashanti is my type, for the reason that Ashanti is yet unspoilt by the bad methods of the missionary.

" I remember once seeing Rev. Ramsay in Kumasi. He told me he had laboured in Ashanti off and on for forty years. I asked how many Ashantis he had in his church at Kumasi proper ? He said, thirty. His assistant corrected him and said fifty. I asked him how many in all Ashanti ?, About two hundred. Not quite so many, his assistant concurring. Rev. Asare, the assistant, and his good wife are both Africans, who have adopted the European habit. I had visited the missionaries in my African costume. They agreed, including my African friends, that it was appropriate. I hope the object lesson was not without significance to the hopes of the success of their mission. But, however that may be, to-day the Ashanti goes unconcerned of the white man's religion and of the white man's ways, as ancient Egypt might have done.

" What is religion ? If it is that which links back the finite to the infinite, the material to the spiritual, the temporal to the eternal—that which inspires an unfaltering faith in a life beyond the grave, then, I maintain, that the African, in his system of philosophy, gives place to none.

"Hark! What are those suggestive words I catch from the so-called Fetish chant that the priest, called to attend a dying man, is humming in a low, doleful voice!

> ' *Midan, Nyami, Kwiaduampon,*
> *Midan, Nyami, Kwiadu,*
> *Nyami ama, Nyami ama*
> *Nyami na wama mi akom !'*

Meaning :

> ' On God I depend, the impregnable Rock;
> On God I depend, the impregnable Rock.
> God has given, God has given,
> God has given me the priesthood.'

I have loosely rendered the word ' *Kwiaduampon* ' as ' the impregnable rock,' but etymologically, it conveys the idea of ' the ever faithful God.'

" Now, when, in the face of all this you tell the so-called pagan that he will not end well, that he is the devil's own, he listens curiously, and wonders whether you can mean all you say. His attitude henceforth is a defensive one, seldom antagonistic. Henceforth he only asks to be let alone. And yet people wonder that so-called spiritual work makes such little headway in these parts. And the land had rest forty years. Do you not see the purport of it all? It has not pleased the gods to disturb her. Leave her in peace, the slumbering sphinx, until the God of Ethiopia wakes her up! For it is not so much religion that she wants as knowledge—knowledge that will enable her to explain to the waiting world the faith that is in her and the reason of her being.

" According to Dr. Freeman, in his History of Europe, the word pagan originally meant a countryman, and, by extension, a worshipper of false gods. Well, Paul, before the application of the phrase, spoke of a temple with the inscription ' to the *unknown* God,' whom men ignorantly worshipped. Evident, therefore, it is that a pagan is not necessarily a worshipper of false gods. Even Marcus Aurelius persecuted the Christians; yet it is conceivable that had he lived in a later age, he would have set his philosophical sayings in terms of Christianity.

" If Christ and God are one, those who worship God ignorantly, worship Christ ignorantly, and it were better for the many to worship in spirit and in truth that which they know fully, but as it were through a glass darkly, rather than don the intellectual garb which ends in questioning the Divinity of Christ, and by parity of reasoning, according to the theologians, the Divinity of God.

" In the philosophy of the West African there

is no reason why Christ should not be God. For
to him man is half God and half man. But a
thin veil divides the finite from the infinite, and
when Death pulls aside the curtain, there is no
knowing what one shall be. Indeed, it is conceivable that paganism, scientifically interpreted,
may place the Christ on a higher pedestal than
Christianity has yet done. What the unspoilt
educated African feels he wants is, rest—rest to
think out his own thoughts, and to work out his
own salvation.

" Have we, who advocate these views, lost faith
in Christianity? It does not follow. It was Dr.
Blyden who wrote in the ' Significance of Liberia '
these remarkable words : . . . . ' I am sure
that Christianity, as conceived and modified in
Europe and America, with its oppressive
hierarchy, its caste prejudices and limitations, its
pecuniary burdens and exactions, its injurious
intermeddling in the harmless and useful customs
of alien peoples, is not the Christianity of Christ.
But I am sure, also, that the Christianity of Christ
is no cunningly devised fable, no *ignis fatuus*, to
disappear in darkness and confusion. I am sure
that its spirit will ultimately prevail in the pro-
ceedings of men; that the knowledge of the Lord
shall cover the earth as the waters cover the sea.
I am sure that Jesus, upon whom is the spirit of
the Lord, because He hath anointed Him to preach

the gospel to the poor, to heal the broken-hearted, to preach deliverance to the captive, the recovery of sight to the blind, to set at liberty them that are bruised; I am sure that this

> " Jesus shall reign where'er the sun
> Doth his successive journeys run ! "

I am sure, also, that all counterfeits, however bright or real they look, must vanish as the truth appears. We should not be discouraged because the system bearing the name of Christ makes no progress on this Continent—that it lingers, halts, and limps on the threshold of the great opportunity. Jesus is lame. He has been wounded in the house of his friends. We must bind up his wounds. Treading in the footsteps of our immortal countryman, we must bear the Cross after Jesus. We must strip him of the useless, distorting, and obstructive habiliments by which he has been invested by the materialising sons of Japhet. Let Him be lifted up as he really is, that He may be seen, pure and simple, by the African, and He will draw all men unto Him ! '

" The broader outlook upon religion is the lot of the careless Ethiopian. He need not necessarily see God except through Christ, but is, withal, so Catholic that he can speak of the universal

> ' Strife that won our life
> With the incarnate Son of God.'

" A significant marriage took place in Sierra Leone in March of the present year. A highly cultured African gentleman was married to a Mohammedan lady. Of this lady the *Weekly News* of 21st March, 1908, says : ' There has been no attempt to unmake her, no inducement to make her alter the religion of her fathers or her native dress.' I remember overhearing an argument in a railway carriage between two educated Africans as to the effect of such marriages. They were both Sierra Leone men; and the sore point with one of the controversialists was as to how her ladyship would be received at Government House, or how she would receive at home the friends of her lord and master. Here you have the two warring elements in national development : ' What is it that the white man expects me to do? What is it that I am called upon in reason and by nature to do?' Between these two the manhood of the race is throttled and sacrificed on the altar of convenience.

" Now, what appears remarkable in Sierra Leone would not be remarkable on the Gold Coast, where it is common for educated men to mate with less privileged women. And the reason, founded on common sense, is not far to seek. Between the African woman who, collecting firewood in a plantation, overpowered by nature, brings her little one into the world, soothes it, and carries it safely home with her load and the African lady who talks of going *home*, meaning Europe, to be confined, there is a mighty difference. The latter is the product of an effete system of training, and it and the system will perish out of hand. The former has a foundation in character that will bear the weight of the ages as far as African life and work are concerned.

" With respect to marriage a great blunder has been committed by the meddlesome missionaries, namely, ' that of forcing a life of hypocrisy upon those whom they compass earth and sea to get into the fold. Whereas the average so-called convert was, before he came into the church, living a fairly decent, open, life in his marital relations, embracing Christianity invariably meant for him adopting subterfuges and chicanery to cover up the way of the old life, which not all the spiritual graces could help him to brush aside.'

" There is a vulgar way of approaching the question of polygamy; there is the scientific way; and lastly there is the spiritual way. It may appear strange to the average man that there is a spiritual side to polygamy. Yet on second thought it must be so. In this, as in other matters, evil be to him who evil thinks.

" The crux of the educational question, as it affects the African, is that Western methods denationalise him. He becomes a slave to foreign ways of life and thought. He will desire to be a slave no longer. So far is this true that the moment the unspoilt educated African shows initiative and asserts an individuality, his foreign mentor is irritated by the phenomenon. In September, 1905, public events on the Gold Coast led me to write in the local press as follows : ' We feel, secondly, that the educated native is unduly maligned for party purposes. It is the same cry as the educated Welsh, Irish, or Scotch. In any case, it is a childish cry—a sign of weakness. Does a native cease to be a native when once he is educated ? . . . . But for the educated native, where would the unsophisticated native be ? Hence the weakness of the cry—the shibboleth of the ' educated native.' Heaven grant that the educated native may never be wanting in his duty to his less privileged brethren, or betray their trust in him.'

" But let there be no mistake about the matter. The foregoing strictly applies to the unspoilt cultured African. The other type is no good to anybody. The superfine African gentleman, who, at the end of every second or third year, talks of a run to Europe, lest there should be a nervous breakdown, may be serious or not, but is bound in time to be refined off the face of the African continent.

" And now I come to the question of questions :

' How may the West African be trained so as to preserve his national identity and race instincts ? '

" As a precautionary measure, I would take care to place the educational seminary in a region far beyond the reach of the influence of the coast. If I were founding a national University for the Gold Coast and for Ashanti, I would make a suitable suburb of Kumasi the centre. But why do I speak of a national University? For the simple reason that you cannot educate a people unless you have a suitable training ground. A Tuskegee Institute is very useful in its way, but where would you get the teachers unless you drew them from the ranks of the University trained men? And since even the teachers must be first locally trained, the highest training ground becomes a necessity.

" I would found in such a University a Chair for History; and the kind of history that I would teach would be universal history with particular reference to the part Ethiopia has played in the affairs of the world. I would lay stress upon the fact that while Rameses II. was dedicating temples to ' the God of gods and secondly to his own glory,' the God of the Hebrews had not yet appeared unto Moses in the burning bush; that Africa was the cradle of the world's systems and philosophies, and the nursing mother of its religions. In short, that Africa has nothing to be ashamed of of its place among the nations of the earth. I would make it possible for this seat of learning to be the means of revising erroneous current ideas regarding the African; of raising him in self-respect; and of making him an efficient co-worker in the uplifting of man to nobler effort.

" Then I should like to see professorships for the study of the Fanti, Hausa, and Yoruba languages. The idea may seem odd upon the first view. But if you are inclined to regard it thus, I can only point to the examples of Ireland and Denmark, who have found the vehicle of a national language much the safest and most natural way of national conservancy and evolution. If the Dane and Irish find it expedient in Europe, surely the matter is worthy of consideration by the African. Says Mr. James O'Hannay, writing on the work of the Irish League and the influence of a national language in the November, 1905, number of the *Independent Review*, at pages 311 and 312 : ' Our history, our customs, our characters are unintelligible to us until we know it. Character, for instance, is the result of inheritance and environment; and there is no more subtly influential environment than the language we speak. If these two are in opposition, if a people inherits a Celtic spirit and grows up in an Anglo-Saxon atmosphere, with the English language on its lips, what kind of character will result? It is likely

that a people tossed in this cross sideway of contradictions will tend to develop inconsistencies of
character—amazing force rendered useless by
recurring spasms of weakness, brilliant intellectual capacity sterilised by inability to grasp the
conditions of material progress, and so forth.'

" If you want a further support to this view,
you have it laid down in an interview with Mr.
A. G. Fraser (Trinity College, Oxford), the
Principal of Trinity College, Kandy, Ceylon.
Says the *Times* reporter : ' He laid special stress
on the importance of conducting the training
given in Indian Colleges on a vernacular basis
rather than through the medium of English, as is
too often the case at present.   The system existing
in most missionary and Government schools tends
distinctly to separate those thus educated from
their own race.   He advocated education almost
on Japanese lines, *i.e.*, thorough teaching of
English as a subject and literature, but the teaching of science, engineering, medicine, etc., through
the medium of the vernacular, and not of English
—with a complete connection between the village
school and the central college.'

" Moreover, I would make this seat of learning
so renowned and attractive that students from the
United States, the West Indies, Sierra Leone, and
Liberia, as well as from Lagos and the Gambia,
would flock to it.   And they would come to this

Mecca—this *alma mater* of national conservancy, not in top hat and broad cloth, but in the sober garb in which the Romans conquered the material world, and in which we may conquer the spiritual world.

" Now, it is easy to see that the graduates that such a school will turn out will be *men*—no effete, mongrel, product of foreign systems.

" When three or four years back I had the pleasure of accompanying Dr. Blyden to the Royal Academy, he drew my particular attention to a famous picture, representing the wolf and the lamb as dwelling together, etc. After we had both drunk in the beauty of portraiture for a while, he gravely remarked : ' And a little child shall lead them—that is Africa.' I was struck by the allusion, and I still think there is a deal in the reflection. But it has since struck me also, that it is not the spoilt educated African that may be expected to help in the regenerative work of the world. The unspoilt son of the tropics, nursed in a tropical atmosphere, favourable to the growth of national life, he it is who may show us the way.

" The voice of the ancient universal God goes forth once more, who will go for us, who will show us any good? May there be a full, free, and hearty response from the sons of Ethiopia in the four quarters of the globe.' '

CHAPTER XIX.

A *SIMILITUDE*: THE GREEK AND THE FANTI.

CHAPTER XIX.

A Similitude : The Greek and the Fanti.

By this time the precocious youth was well on in his teens, and was already grappling with the intricacies of Greek roots and Latin suffixes. But often would his father warn him to be mindful more of the things which matter, as he quaintly put it. Now and again he would induce the youth to draw comparisons between the mode of thought and the practice of the ancients; and he would insist that there was no better intellectual, moral, and national training for a young Fanti than such exercise involved. By way of encouragement, when the youth had done particularly well, he would take him upon new ground and delight him with stories from Homer's great masterpiece, which, in a curious way, reflected the every-day life of their own people.

On this particular occasion, you may well imagine the excitement of Ekra Kwow, as he drew a low stool beside the paterfamilias, all eagerness for the latter to begin. The youth looked disappointed, as, instead of beginning a story, his father continued smoking, and simply thrust into

his hand an old, well-thumbed popular edition of
the story of the Odyssey, done into beautiful
English by the Rev. Alfred J. Church.

"What is the matter, father; are you not well
to-night?"

"That's not it, my boy. I am as well as ever,
thank you. But to-night I want you to read to me
instead. I want to see how you handle Mr.
Church's beautiful setting of the great thoughts
of the master. You know to some this feast of the
gods is like throwing pearls before swine. But
go on. Begin with the visit of Athené to
Nausicaa, the daughter of King Alcinoüs."

Thus the youth began : " Athené spake, saying,
why hath thy mother so careless a child, Nausicaa?
Lo! thy raiment lieth unwashed, and yet the day
of thy marriage is at hand, when thou must have
fine clothing for thyself, and to give to them that
shall lead thee to thy bridegroom's house; for thus
doth a bride win good repute. Do thou, therefore,
arise with the day, and go to wash the raiment,
and I will go with thee .   .   .

" And when the morning was come, Nausicaa
awoke, marvelling at the dream, and went seeking
her parents. Her mother she found busy with
her maidens at the loom, spinning yarn dyed with
purple of the sea, and her father she met as he
was going to the Council with the Chiefs of the
land. Then she said : ' Give me, Father, the

wagon with the mules that I may take the garments to the river to wash them ' . . . .

" Then he called to the men, and they made
ready the wagon, and harnessed the mules; and
the maiden brought the raiment out of her chamber
and put it in the wagon. Also her mother filled
a basket with all manner of food, and poured wine
in a goat-skin bottle. Olive oil also she gave her,
that Nausicaa and her maidens might anoint themselves after the bath. And Nausicaa took the
reins and touched the mules with the whip. Then
was there a clatter of hoofs, and the mules went
on with their load, nor did they grow weary."²

As the youth stopped for a second to take
breath, Kwamankra exclaimed, " That's good.
Does that remind you of anything you see daily
around you ? "

The youth paused for a moment, and then said :
" It looks very much like how the Fanti women
prepare to do their washing in the brook, and it is
curious the mention of the use of oil to anoint the
body after a bath. Why, that's just what our
people do."

" Good; powers of observation fair, my boy,"
remarked Kwamankra proudly. " You see in
these extra-civilised days the laundress and the
charwoman do the cleansing of our soiled linen,
and who would dream of seeing a king's daughter
doing her own washing, let alone her father's, or

her brother's.   Yet, in ancient Greece it was not
so.   The highest in birth preserved native simplicity, much as the unspoilt among our own people
do unto this day.   Then there are just one or two
points you have missed in the narrative.   Alcinoüs
is described as a king.   His daughter meets him
as he is going to the Council with the chiefs of the
land.   There is something strikingly in accord
with our own custom here—just what an *Omanhin*
would do."

" Lo ! thy raiment lieth unwashed, and yet the
day of thy marriage is at hand, when thou must
have fair clothing for thyself, *and to give to them
that shall lead thee to thy bridegroom's house*," he
quoted, and then added, " thus do we in marriage
and in death provide for the kinsmen and the kins-
women who lead us."

As the youth began to understand what the
paterfamilias had meant by " the things which
matter," he read with far greater expression the
inimitable passages which describe the meeting of
Ulysses with Nausicaa, her kindly address and
hospitality, and his introduction to the Court of
King Alcinoüs.   And such a Court !   " A
wondrous place it was, with walls of brass and
doors of gold, hanging on posts of silver; and on
either side of the door were dogs of gold and silver,
the work of Hephæstus and against the wall all
along from the threshold to the inner chamber,

were set seats, on which sat the chiefs of the
Phæacians feasting; and youths wrought in gold
stood holding torches in their hands, to give light
in the darkness. Fifty women were in the house
grinding corn and weaving robes, for the women
of the land are no less skilled to weave than are
the men to sail the sea. And round about the
house were gardens beautiful exceedingly, with
orchards of fig, and apple, and pear, and pome-
granate, and olive. Drought hurts them not, nor
frost, and harvest comes after harvest without
ceasing. Also there was a vineyard; and some of
the grapes were parching in the sun, and some
were being gathered, and some again were but just
turning red. And there were beds of all manner
of flowers; and in the midst of all were two
fountains which never failed."

"And yet," observed Kwamankra, "the
daughter of King Alcinoüs was not above cleansing soiled linen; and there is something sweetly
simple and familiar, as you see Ulysses bidden
unto the feast, and an attendant pours water on
his hands, and he is given meat and drink there-
after, and in all this the Fanti-born feels himself
particularly at home with these Grecians."

"Indeed," pursued Kwamankra, "as one turns
over the wonderful pages of the story of the
Odyssey, he stumbles across such similitudes of

thought and action, as between the Greek and the
Fanti, that are simply amazing."

" Tell me all about that," snapped up the youth
eagerly.

" Well," continued Kwamankra, " in no phase
of Grecian thought is this more striking than in
the conception of the Deity. The great *Niak-
rapon*, or *Nyami*, of the Fanti corresponds with the
Zeus of the Greek, as *Abusum* correspond with the
lesser gods; and when the Greek speaks of the
' oracle of the god in the midst of an oak tree,' he
conveys the same idea as the Fanti does when he
speaks of the *busum* in an *odoom* tree, popularly
described as fetish.   Again, similarly, when the
Fanti makes an invocation, it is upon *Nyiakrapon*
he calls, ' *Mika Nyiakrapon*,' as distinguished
from any of the *Abusum*, or lesser gods, just in the
same way as the Greek would say, ' Would to
God,' as distinguished from any of the lesser gods.
Moreover, the spiritual sense of the Greek was as
keen as that of the Fanti.   The gods of the Fanti
mix to-day as freely with mortals as did Proteus,
Poseidon, or Athené, the daughter of Zeus; and
their offices are the same, for, if men paid heed,
they would still gather inspiration for action as
in the days when Athené came down from
Olympus, and said unto doubting Ulysses, ' Verily,
thou art weak in faith.   Some put their trust in
men, yet men are weaker than the gods; why

trustest not thou in me?   Verily, I am with thee, and will keep thee to the end.   But now sleep, for to watch all the night is vexation of spirit.' "

"Why," quoth the youth, "that reads like a passage in the Bible."

"Yes," the thinker went on musingly; "God hath not spoken to man only in the Hebrew Scriptures.   But I was going to say, and so one might go on almost *ad infinitum*, gathering pearls of thought at every turn.   Take, for instance, the incident when Penelope says to Eumæus, 'Call now this stranger; didst thou not mark how my son sneezed a blessing when I spake?'   I do not know whether the idea of sneezing a blessing occurs in any other language; but a Fanti says : '*Akam yey*' when you sneeze in his presence, exactly expressing the same idea.   Again, the customs of offering sacrifice to the gods, and making libation to gods and deceased ancestors, are common alike to the two peoples.   And when you recall the familiar way in which the poet speaks of Eurybates, the herald of Ulysses, 'Older than he, dark-skinned, round in the shoulders, with curly hair,' it dawns upon the Ethiopian that he gains vastly more in self-respect by intimate acquaintance with the ancient Greek than with the modern Saxon.

Let nothing be done through strife or vain-glory; but
in lowliness of mind let each esteem others better
than themselves.

Look not every man on his own things, but every man
also on the things of others.

Let this mind be in you, which was also in Christ
Jesus:

Who, being in the form of God, thought it not robbery
to be equal with God:

But made himself of no reputation,

And took upon him the form of a servant,

And was made in the likeness of men.

And being found in fashion as a man, he humbled himself, and became obedient unto death, even the death
of the Cross.

WHEREFORE

God also hath highly exalted him,

And given him a name

Which is above every name,

That at the name of Jesus

Every knee should bow;

Of things in heaven,

And things in earth,

And things under the earth;

And that every tongue should confess that Jesus Christ
is Lord, to the glory of God the Father.—PAUL.

    *   *   *   *   *

The tumult and the shouting dies;

The Captains and the Kings depart:

Still stands thine ancient sacrifice,

A humble and a contrite heart.

Lord God of Hosts, be with us yet,

Lest we forget—lest we forget!—KIPLING.

CHAPTER XX.

AND A LITTLE CHILD SHALL LEAD THEM.

By the year 1925 a mighty change had come over
the thought of the nations, and it was due to some
extent to the work of the *Gold Coast Nation and
Ethiopian Review,* promoted by Kwamankra just
before the close of the first ten years of the century
in the interests of Gold Coast national conservancy; but as time went on it had broadened
out in sympathy to embrace the needs of the entire
race. During the preceding fifteen years the
Nation had freely circulated throughout the
Ethiopian world, and the promoter and the
Editors were in constant communication with the
leading thinkers of the race throughout the world.
Moreover, it had gradually dawned upon
workers and thinkers alike that the way of
material argument—the argument of bomb and
shell—was not the Ethiopian's way, and, in the
world of progressive thought, the lamb was, after
all, as the seer had foretold, leading the wolf and
the lion instincts of the nations into right

channels. It was a moral force with a moral persuasiveness which, like the wind, blowing whence men know not, yet was moulding the spiritual atmosphere of the world. For what was to have become a great race war had become a mighty truce. The black races had at length learnt to run along their own natural lines of development, and the white needed the black and the black needed the white. The work of Cain had given place to the grace of conciliation, and the West had called to the South and the South had responded in the thundering words of the great thinker, who said : " But if we fail in this? —If blinded by the gain of the moment we see nothing in our dark man but a vast engine of labour; if to us he is not a man, but only a tool; if dispossessed entirely of the land for which he now shows that rare aptitude for peasant proprietorship for the lack of which among their masses many great nations are decaying; if we force him permanently in his millions into the locations and compounds and slums of our cities, obtaining his labour cheaper, but to lose what the wealth of five rands could not return to us; if uninstructed in the highest forms of labour, without the rights of citizenship, his own social organisation broken up without our having aided him to participate in our own; if unbound to us by gratitude and sympathy and alien to us in blood and colour, we reduce this vast mass to the condition of a great, seething, ignorant proletariat—then I would rather draw a veil over the future of this land.''

To sentiments such as these, ringing with deep sincerity and earnestness, workers and leaders on the Ethiopian platform could not but respond with equal sincerity and earnestness; and, in the mutual respect and confidence which resulted, the black man could call to the white man and say :

" Lofty I stand from each sister land, patient and wearily
    wise,
    With the weight of a world of sadness in my quiet
        passionless eyes,
    Dreaming alone of a people, dreaming alone of a day
    When men shall not rape my riches and curse me and
        go away;
    Making a bawd of my bounty, fouling the hand that
        gave—
    Till I rise in my wrath and I sweep on their path and
        I stamp them into a grave.
    Dreaming of men who will bless me, of women esteem-
        ing me good,
    Of children born in my borders, of radiant motherhood,
    Of cities leaping to stature, of fame like a flag unfurled
    As I pour the tide of my riches in the eager lap of the
        world.''

Yes, it was a holy truce, and it was the spirit of humility which sealed it.   It was one of those startling truths of life which men scarce realise when they hear it uttered. The late Henry Drummond emphasised this lesson in modern times in a way few had done before. And yet he taught nothing new in this respect. To toil and moil for reputation, fortune, or position, and, when gained, to wonder at one's folly at having wasted so much energy and so much precious time is as old as the days of King Solomon who, in the plenitude of his power and might and dominion, wrote all down as vanity. And the converse way of life is as old as Socrates and the Pyramids; and Ethiopia can afford to take her part ungrudgingly in the arduous task of advancing humanity. The wonder is that, twenty centuries after Christ, the leading nations have not yet learnt this great, yet simple, truth. And so it happens that they still toil and moil to make proselytes of other nations only to fill them with the unrest from which they suffer and to weary them with the burden which they bear. After years of patient waiting and discipline, Japan has at length shaken herself free from ancient conservatism, and China is following suit. As for India, she is even now in the grip of a great delirium. The lion and the bear are being threatened in their lair, and men can hardly believe their senses. And yet this is not the better part of Japan which wise men would wish to see perpetuated. Perhaps no one person, living or dead, did more to reveal the East unto the West than the late Lafcadio Hearn; and nowhere did the master-hand wield the magic wand more powerfully than in the living pages of that remarkable work, *Kokoro*, which "treats of the inner rather than of the outer life of Japan." And herein lay the power of our author. He treated of the inner things of life. He belonged to that band of men who force their fellow-men to think. They are not always popular; but whether or not, they are the saviours of the race.

Lest the temper of the people of the Gold Coast may be misunderstood, let it be premised that it is a remarkable thing that the date of Japan's political awakening has been noted to synchronise with the political awakening of the Gold Coast. Had the fates been propitious, the development of the latter might have been equally remarkable in its way. It is a curious fact, but one worth recording, that those who had the guidance, or, to use a more correct phrase, the protection of the budding aspirations of Fanti nationality, noted early the symptoms of latent national possibilities, and, acting on the principle of *divide et impero*, scattered the fragments to the winds. But the voice of the Creator has gone forth, and, even as the sea gives up its dead, so will the four winds blow back the hopes that were well nigh lost, and fan them into action. For, remember, that the Gold Coast people were contemporaries and brethren in institutions, language, customs, and practices, in the far interior, of the Ashantis whose polity, prowess and moral backbone have aroused the admiration of the world. For quite a century they were a martial power to reckon with, though without arms of precision; and when measures of repression have been removed, it is quite conceivable that their inherent virility will be turned into healthy channels of statecraft and race development.

It is, perhaps, not generally known that the Denkiras in the Gold Coast, occupying the country this side of the Offin River, whose capital town Gwikwa is close to Cape Coast, were once the masters of the Ashantis. The names of Ampon-saim and Intsim Gakiri of the royal line of Denkira are well-known in the history of Ashanti. There was a time when they inspired terror in the breasts of the Ashantis, and it was the haughty demand of Intsim Gakiri that the Ashanti tribute for a given year should be accompanied by a tooth of the king and his " best " wife that roused the Ashantis to the deadly struggle with the Denkiras which ended in the submission of the latter and their subsequent immigration to the Gold Coast, punctuated by a series of other political events.

And if you turn to the Fanti portion of the Gold Coast, you find this, that they were one mighty host who broke away—*ifa wa atsiw*, hence

their name Fanti—from their brethren, the
Ashantis in the hinterland and made their way to
the coast. Now, when *Boribori Fanti* came from
Takieman, the *Abura Tuafus* led the van; but they
were then not known as Aburas, no more were the
Anumabus or Akumfis known by their present
designations. They were all, as it has been explained, one mighty host under several great
leaders who sat upon ancient stools in the interior.
Their first care was to secure a suitable habitat for
their gods, *Nanamu.* The god of rain, for
example, was, and is, known as *Nana Yankum.*
The first great centre of the Fantis was *Man-
kessim,* meaning, the great city. As it was
impossible for the hosts of *Boribori Fanti* to abide
together, soon a dispersion took place. It was
reported among those who remained behind of
those who went in the direction of Abura : " *Wo
dzi hwon tsir abura mu nu hu,*" that was to say,
" they have taken some direction unknown," the
name *Abura* attaching to the people from the verb
abura. Likewise the Akumfis were so called from
the density of the multitude, *Kumkumfi,* which
separated from the main body and settled in the
district now known as Akumfi.

The polity of these people has been eloquently
described by competent Fanti writers, and in the
pages of their works is seen a system of government at once harmonious, progressive, and

sympathetic — a system capable of infinite
development.

Moreover, in the language of these people are
certain characteristic root ideas. It is the
language of poetry, and their unrecorded songs are
full of the deep meanings constituting the soul of
life. Take, for example, the word "*wireh*,"
meaning heart affection, in the phrase "*miwireh
akitawu*," that is to say, "my heart is firmly knit
to your heart." So familiar are they with the
essence of the Godhead that you have ascriptions
such as *Onumankuma*, meaning "*Onu a obotum de
oka de Madaku ma*," that is to say, "he who can
say, I alone am the giver," clearly corresponding
to the eternal Giver of all good. Take another
ascription, *Kwerampon*, meaning "*ekwerina
ebira pun wa onye*," that is to say, "if you lean
against him, none can sever you," clearly carrying
the idea of "none can pluck you out of my hands."
Now, whence these root ideas? They cannot be
merely fortuitous, traceable, as they are, to the
innermost consciousness of the people.

Thus it will be seen that the Gold Coast people
are as good an Eastern type in some respects as
those of whom we have written. Yet, to-day,

"Lofty she stands from each sister land patient and
wearily wise."

with a patience that marks for leadership in the
spiritual realm.

Undoubtedly the highest form of character development attainable in any religion is that set forth in the graphic portraiture of Paul of Tarsus, where he makes true humility the door to the highest honour. And who can doubt it that, in this respect, Ethiopia, among the nations, typifies this aspect of the developed character to-day more than any other ?   In order to carry on her mission of peace what is wanted is the opportunity of inter-communication; and it is conceivable that some day it may be possible to reach Lake Chad from Northern Nigeria, and Kumasi to become a great centre for converging lines of the Cape to Cairo railway. When that eventuality happens, and Ethiopia will have entered upon her universal spiritual mission, then, hoary with age, and freed from the trammels of so-called world progress, aims, and ambitions, she shall pursue her onward path to God in the way of humble service to mankind; and, so, the saying of the seer shall become true that " A little child shall lead them."

FINIS.

171220-100-6-60W